A Barrel of Fun

A Barrel of Fun

J. John & Mark Stibbe

MONARCH
BOOKS

Mill Hill, London & Grand Rapids, Michigan

First published in the UK in 2003 by Monarch Books,
Concorde House, Grenville Place,
Mill Hill, London NW7 3SA.

Illustrations by Darren Harvey Regan

Distributed by:
UK: STL, PO Box 300, Kingstown Broadway, Carlisle,
Cumbria CA3 0QS;
USA: Kregel Publications, PO Box 2607,
Grand Rapids, Michigan 49501.

ISBN 1 85424 621 6 (UK)
ISBN 0 8254 6220 7 (USA)

British Library Cataloguing Data
A catalogue record for this book is available
from the British Library.

Book design and production for the publishers by
Gazelle Creative Productions Ltd,
Concorde House, Grenville Place, Mill Hill, London NW7 3SA.

Note to church magazine editors

Permission to use up to 750 words from this volume is granted free of charge for reproduction in church magazines and newsletters when produced on a non-commercial basis. Please acknowledge source in the following form: From *A Barrel of Fun*, J. John and Mark Stibbe, Monarch Books.

Preface

This is the third volume that we have put together of stories, sayings, illustrations and quotes. Our prayer is that you will find this volume enjoyable and that you will also find words of wisdom for your life. We hope you will find riveting stories, thought-provoking parables, as well as humorous anecdotes. We also hope that as well as taking them to heart you will also pass them on!

Wherever we have borrowed, we have tried to give due credit. However, for any material that we may have unconsciously remembered and innocently rewritten, we ask absolution.

This is a book to dip into. It is not meant to be a ladder of logic from one chapter to the next, but a literary bouquet. You choose your flower and wear it that day.

May our Creator God be good to you, all around the compass and the clock.

Mark Stibbe and J. John
St Andrew's Church
Chorleywood
UK
January 2003

Adulthood

> ### "My Resignation…"
>
> I am hereby officially tendering my resignation as an adult. I have decided I would like to accept the responsibilities of an eight-year-old.
>
> I want to go to McDonald's and think that it's a four-star restaurant.
>
> I want to sail sticks across a fresh mud puddle and make a sidewalk with rocks.
>
> I want to think M&Ms are better than money because you can eat them.
>
> I want to lie under a big oak tree and run a lemonade stand with my friends on a hot summer's day.
>
> I want to return to a time when life was simple; when all you knew were colours, multiplication tables, and nursery rhymes, but that didn't bother you, because you didn't know what you didn't know and you didn't care.
>
> All you knew was to be happy because you were blissfully unaware of all the things that should make you worried or upset.
>
> I want to think the world is fair. That everyone is honest and good.
>
> I want to believe that anything is possible. I want to be oblivious to the complexities of life and be overly excited by the little things again.
>
> I want to live simple again. I don't want my day to consist of computer crashes, mountains of paperwork, depressing news, how to survive more days in the month than there is money in the bank, doctor bills, gossip, illness, and loss of loved ones.
>
> I want to believe in the power of smiles, hugs, a kind word, truth, justice, peace, dreams, the imagination, mankind, and making angels in the snow.
>
> So… here's my chequebook and my car-keys, and my credit card bills. I am officially resigning from adulthood.

Age

The first half of our lives we're romantic. The second half we're rheumatic.

The old believe everything; the middle-aged suspect everything; the young know everything.
Oscar Wilde

Education is the best provision for old age.
Aristotle

A minister visits an elderly woman from his congregation. As he sits on the couch he notices a large bowl of peanuts on the coffee table. "Mind if I have a few?" he asks.

"No, not at all!" the woman replies.

They talk for an hour and as the minister stands to leave, he realises that instead of eating just a few peanuts, he has emptied the bowl.

"I'm terribly sorry for eating all your peanuts, I really only meant to eat a few."

"Oh, that's all right," the woman says. "Ever since I lost my teeth all I can do is suck the chocolate off them."

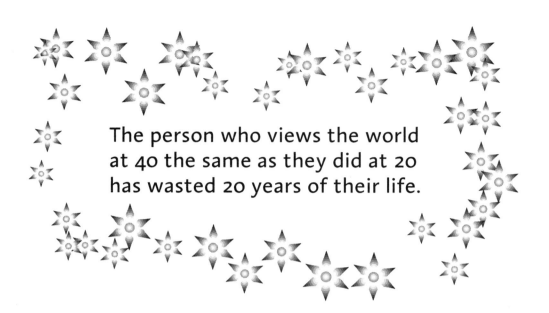

The person who views the world at 40 the same as they did at 20 has wasted 20 years of their life.

Nurse: How old are you, Mrs Smith?

Patient: None of your business.

Nurse: But the doctor must know your age for his records.

Patient: Well, first, multiply twenty by two, then add ten. Got that?

Nurse: Yes. Fifty.

Patient: All right, now subtract fifty, and tell me, what do you get?

Nurse: Zero.

Patient: Right. And that's exactly the chance of me telling you my age.

Grandma and Grandpa were sitting outside watching the beautiful sunset and reminiscing about "the good old days", when Grandma turned to Grandpa and said, "Darling, do you remember when we first started dating and you used to just casually reach over and take my hand?" Grandpa looked over at her, smiled and took her aged hand in his.

With a wry little smile Grandma pressed a little farther, "Darling, do you remember how after we were engaged you'd sometimes lean over and suddenly kiss me on the cheek?" Grandpa leaned slowly toward Grandma and gave her a lingering kiss on her wrinkled cheek.

Growing bolder still, Grandma said, "Darling, do you remember how, after we were first married, you'd kind of nibble on my ear?" Grandpa slowly got up from his rocker and headed into the house. Alarmed, Grandma said, "Darling, where are you going?"

Grandpa replied, "To get my teeth!"

A 17th Century Nun's Prayer about Old Age

Lord, thou knowest better than I know myself that I am growing older and will some day be old.

Keep me from the fatal habit of thinking I must say something on every subject and on every occasion.

Release me from craving to straighten out everybody's affairs.

Make me thoughtful but not moody; helpful but not bossy.

With my vast store of wisdom it seems a pity not to use it all, but Thou knowest Lord, that I want a few friends at the end.

Keep my mind free from the recital of endless details; give me wings to get to the point.

Seal my lips on my aches and pains. They are increasing and love of rehearsing them is becoming sweeter as the years go by.

I dare not ask for grace enough to enjoy the tales of others' pains, but help me to endure them with patience.

I dare not ask for improved memory, but for a growing humility and a lessening cocksureness when my memory seems to clash with the memories of others. Teach me the glorious lesson that occasionally I may be mistaken.

Keep me reasonably sweet; I do not want to be a saint – some of them are so hard to live with – but a sour old person is one of the crowning works of the Devil.

Give me the ability to see good things in unexpected places and talents in unexpected people.

And, give me, O Lord, the grace to tell them so.

Amen.

Alcohol

The wise old Mother Superior was dying. The nuns gathered around her bed, trying to make her comfortable. They gave her some warm milk to drink, but she refused it.

Then one nun took the glass back to the kitchen. Remembering a bottle of whiskey received as a gift the previous Christmas, she opened it and poured a generous amount into the warm milk.

Back at Mother Superior's bed, she held the glass to her lips. Mother drank a little, then a little more, then before they knew it, she had drunk the whole glass down to the last drop.

"Mother, Mother," the nuns cried, "give us some wisdom before you die!"

She raised herself up in bed with a pious look on her face and pointing out the window said, "Don't sell that cow!"

A new Christian confessed to having a problem with alcohol. She said, "It goes straight to my head."

She was nervous about taking Holy Communion for the first time because even a sip of wine would make her tipsy.

After the service, she told the minister that her fears had been unfounded.

"What happened?" asked the leader.

She replied, "It went straight to my heart."

Angels

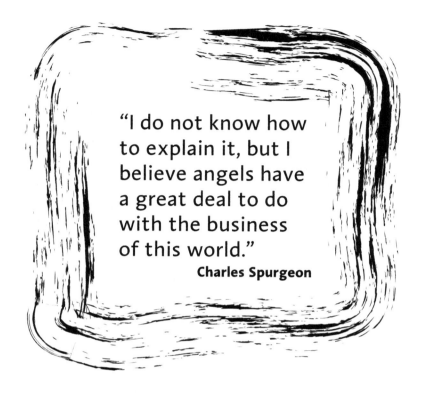

"I do not know how to explain it, but I believe angels have a great deal to do with the business of this world."

Charles Spurgeon

A Norwegian missionary, Marie Monsen, in China in the early 20th century, testified to the intervention of angels when Christians were in great danger. They had taken refuge in the mission compound only to be surrounded by looting soldiers and they were astonished to find that they were left in peace. A few days later the hostile men explained that they were ready to break down the flimsy wall when they noticed tall soldiers with shining faces on a high roof in the compound. Marie Monsen wrote, "The heathen saw them, it was a testimony to them, but they were invisible to us."

Anger

"He that would be angry and not sin, must be angry at nothing but sin."
Revd William Secker (17th century)

"An angry man is again angry with himself when he returns to reason."
Publius Syrus

"Anyone can be angry. That is easy. But to be angry with the right person, to the right degree, at the right time, for the right purpose, and in the right way – that is not easy."
Aristotle

Anger is one letter removed from Danger.

Never answer a letter while you're angry.
Chinese proverb

People who fly into a rage always make a bad landing.

Anger makes your mouth work faster than your mind.

Apathy

> "Science may have found a cure for most evils, but it has found no remedy for the worst of them all – the apathy of human beings."
>
> **Helen Keller (1880–1968)**

Apologetics

A divinity school invited one of the greatest minds to lecture in the theological education centre. One year, the guest lecturer was a professor, who spoke for two and a half hours "proving" that the resurrection of Jesus was false.

The professor quoted scholar after scholar and book after book. He concluded that since there was no such thing as the historical resurrection, the religious tradition of the church was groundless, emotional mumbo-jumbo, because it was based on a relationship with a risen Jesus, who, in fact, never rose from the dead in any literal sense. He then asked if there were any questions.

After about 30 seconds, an old preacher with a head of woolly white hair stood up in the back of the auditorium.

"Docta Professer, I got one question," he said as all eyes turned towards him. He reached into his lunch sack and pulled out an apple and began eating it. CRUNCH, MUNCH, "My question is a simple question" …CRUNCH, MUNCH… "Now, I ain't never read them books you read" …CRUNCH, MUNCH… "and I can't recite the Scriptures in the original Greek"…CRUNCH, MUNCH… "I don't know nothin' about Niebuhr and Heidegger"…CRUNCH, MUNCH… He finished the apple. "All I wanna know is: This apple I just ate – was it bitter or sweet?"

The professor paused for a moment and answered in exemplary scholarly fashion: "I cannot possibly answer that question, for I haven't tasted your apple."

The white-haired preacher dropped the core of his apple into his crumpled paper bag, looked up at the professor and said calmly, "Neither have you tasted my Jesus."

The 1,000 plus in attendance could not contain themselves. The auditorium erupted with applause and cheers. The professor thanked his audience and promptly left the platform.

B

Bible

> They lie on the table side by side
> The Holy Bible and the TV Guide.
> One is well worn and cherished with pride.
> Not the Bible, but the TV Guide.
> One is used daily to help folks decide.
> No, not the Bible, but the TV Guide.
> As the pages are turned, what shall they see?
> Oh, what does it matter, turn on the TV.
> So they open the book in which they confide.
> No, not the Bible, but the TV Guide.
> The Word of God is seldom read.
> Maybe a verse before they fall into bed.
> Exhausted and sleepy and tired as can be.
> Not from reading the Bible, from watching TV.
> So then back to the table side by side,
> Lie the Holy Bible and the TV Guide.
> No time for prayer, no time for the Word,
> The plan of Salvation is seldom heard.
> But forgiveness of sin, so full and free,
> Is found in the Bible, not on TV.

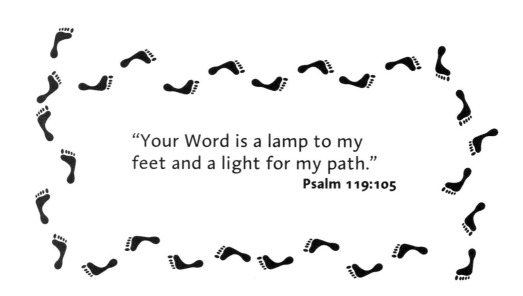

"Your Word is a lamp to my feet and a light for my path."

Psalm 119:105

"*If you are suffering from tooth decay you should consult your dentist. If you are suffering from truth decay, you should consult your Bible.*"
Mark Stibbe

BIBLE STATISTICS

Number of books in the Bible: 66

Chapters: 1,189

Verses: 31,101

Words: 783,137

Letters: 3,566,480

Number of promises given in the Bible: 1,260

Commands: 6,468

Predictions: over 8,000

Fulfilled prophecy: 3,268 verses

Unfulfilled prophecy: 3,140

Number of questions: 3,294

Longest name: Mahershalalhashbaz (Isaiah 8:1)

Longest verse: Esther 8:9 (72 words)

Shortest verse: John 11:35 (2 words: "Jesus wept")

Middle books: Micah and Nahum

Middle verse: Psalm 118:8

Middle chapter: Psalm 117

Shortest chapter (by number of words): Psalm 117

Longest book: Psalms (150 chapters)

Shortest book (by number of words): 3 John

Longest chapter: Psalm 119 (176 verses)

Number of times the word "God" appears: 3,358

Number of times the word "Lord" appears: 7,736

Number of different authors: 40

Number of languages the Bible has been translated into: over 1,200

ittle Johnny had bought Grandma a book for her birthday and wanted to write a suitable inscription. He racked his brain until suddenly he remembered that his father had a book with an inscription of which he was very proud, so Johnny decided to copy it. You can imagine Grandma's surprise when she opened her book, a Bible, and found neatly inscribed the following phrase: "To Grandma, with the compliments of the author."

Billboards

One liners that have appeared outside churches:

"Give God what's right, not what's left"

"A lot of kneeling will leave you in good standing"

"Are you wrinkled with burdens? Come to the church for a faith-lift"

"Don't wait for six strong men to take you to church"

"This church is prayer-conditioned"

"Plan ahead – it wasn't raining when Noah built the ark"

"Merry Christmas to our Christian friends
Happy Hanukkah to our Jewish friends
And to our atheist friends, good luck"

Boasting

A boastful American was being shown the sights of London by a taxi driver.

"What's that building there?" asked the American.

"That's the Tower of London, sir," replied the taxi driver.

"Say, we can put up buildings like that in two weeks," drawled the Texan.

A little while later he said, "And what's that building we're passing now?"

"That's Buckingham Palace, sir, where the Queen lives."

"Is that so?" said the Texan. "Do you know back in Texas we could put a place like that up in a week?"

A few minutes later they were passing Westminster Abbey. The American asked again,

"Hey cabbie, what's that building over there?"

"I'm afraid I don't know, sir," replied the taxi driver. "It wasn't there this morning."

Books

You can't tell a book by its cover.

Some writers create worlds in which the wrongs they suffered as children are finally righted.

"A good book should leave you slightly exhausted at the end. You live several lives while reading it."
William Styron

"Books are ships which pass through the vast seas of time."
Francis Bacon

"There is more treasure in books than in all the pirate's loot in Treasure Island... and best of all, you can enjoy these riches every day."
Walt Disney

What would happen if Moses were alive today? He would come down from Mount Sinai with the Ten Commandments and spend a year trying to get them published.

"Every great book is an action and every great action is a book."
Martin Luther

"A drop of ink may make a million think."
Lord Byron

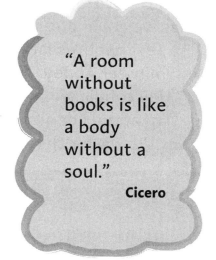

"A room without books is like a body without a soul."
Cicero

"Of making many books there is no end; and much study is a weariness of the flesh."
The Bible, Ecclesiastes 12:12 (AV)

Dear Mr Moses
Thank you for your submission. Unfortunately your material is not suitable for our current publishing needs.
May I remind you that any future submissions must be on paper...

"From the moment I picked your book up until I laid it down I was convulsed with laughter. Some day I intend reading it."

Groucho Marx

A classic is something that everybody wants to have read and nobody wants to read.

Have you heard about the greatest book club in the world? You send them £1 per month for a year and they leave you completely alone!

Cars

> If you MUST speed on the motorway, sing these hymns loudly:
>
> 1. at 45 mph… "God will take care of me"
> 2. at 55 mph… "Guide me, O Thou Great Jehovah"
> 3. at 65 mph… "Nearer my God to Thee"
> 4. at 75 mph… "Nearer still nearer"
> 5. at 85 mph… "This world is not my home"
> 6. at 95 mph… "Lord, I'm coming home"
> 7. at 100 mph… "Precious memories"

"The wheel was man's greatest invention… until he got behind it."
Bill Ireland

"What am I supposed to do with this?" grumbled a motorist as the policeman handed him a speeding ticket.

"Keep it," the policeman said. "When you collect four of them you get a bicycle."

A limo driver is dispatched to the airport to drive the Pope to his hotel.

After getting all Pope John-Paul II's luggage loaded in the limo (and His Holiness doesn't travel light), the driver notices that the Pope is still standing on the curb.

"Excuse me, Your Eminence," says the driver. "Would you please take your seat so we can leave?"

"Well, to tell you the truth," says the Pope, "they never let me drive at the Vatican, and I'd really like to drive today."

"I'm sorry but I cannot let you do that. I'd lose my job! And what if something should happen?" protests the driver, wishing he'd never gone to work that morning.

"There might be something extra in it for you," says the Pope.

Reluctantly, the driver gets in the back as the Pope climbs in behind the wheel. The driver quickly regrets his decision when, after exiting the airport, the Supreme Pontiff floors it, accelerating the limo to 105 mph.

"Please slow down, Your Holiness!" pleads the worried driver, but the Pope keeps the pedal to the metal until they hear sirens.

"Oh, wonderful. Now I'm really going to lose my licence," moans the driver.

The Pope pulls over and rolls down the window as the policeman approaches, but the officer takes one look at him, goes back to his motorcycle, and gets on the radio.

"I need to talk to the Chief," he says to the dispatcher.

The Chief gets on the radio and the officer tells him that he's stopped a limo going 105 mph.

"So bust him," said the Chief.

"I don't think we want to do that – he's really important," said the policeman.

"All the more reason."

"No, I mean really important."

"Who've you got there, the Mayor?"

"Bigger."

"The President?"

"Bigger."

"Well," said the Chief, "who is it?"

"I think it's God!"

"What makes you think it's God?"

"Well, He's got the Pope driving for Him!"

Children

A small boy is sent to bed by his father. Five minutes later...

"Da-ad..."

"What?"

"I'm thirsty. Can you bring me a drink of water?"

"No. You had your chance. Lights out."

Five minutes later: "Da-aaaad..."

"WHAT?"

"I'm THIRSTY. Can I have a drink of water?"

"I told you NO!" If you ask again, I'll have to discipline you!"

Five minutes later... "Daaaa-aaaad..."

"WHAT!"

"When you come in to discipline me, can you bring a drink of water?"

A three-year-old boy went with his dad to see a new litter of kittens. On returning home, he breathlessly informed his mother, "There were two boy kittens and two girl kittens."

"How did you know that?" his mother asked.

"Daddy picked them up and looked underneath," he replied. "I think it's printed on the bottom."

One summer evening during a violent thunderstorm a mother was tucking her son into bed. She was about to turn off the light when he asked with a tremor in his voice, "Mummy, will you sleep in my bed tonight?"

His mother smiled and gave him a reassuring hug. "I can't dear," she said. "I have to sleep in Daddy's room."

A long silence was broken at last by his shaky little voice: "The big sissy."

A six-year-old girl had been so naughty that her mother decided to teach her a lesson. She told her she couldn't go to the school fair.

Then, when the day came, her mother felt she had been too harsh and changed her mind. When she told the little girl she could go to the school fair, the child's reaction was one of gloom and disappointment.

"What's the matter? I thought you'd be glad to go to the school fair," her mother said.

"It's too late!" the little girl said. "I've already prayed for rain, storms and thunder!"

One day, a little boy visited a nurse for a vaccination. After the nurse gave him an injection, she tried to bandage the boy's arm.

"I think you'd better bandage the other arm," he said.

"But, why? I'm supposed to bandage the injected part of your arm to let your friends know not to touch it."

"You really don't know anything about my friends, do you?"

A minister was telling the story of the Prodigal Son and wishing to emphasise the disagreeable attitude of the elder brother on that occasion.

After describing the rejoicing of the household over the return of the prodigal son, he spoke of one who, in the midst of the festivities, failed to share in the joy of the occasion.

"Can anybody," he asked, "tell me who this was?"

A small boy, who had been listening intently to the story, put up his hand.

"I know," he beamed. "It was the fatted calf."

David, aged four, came screaming out of the bathroom to tell his mum that he'd dropped his toothbrush in the toilet. So she fished it out and threw it in the bin.

David stood there thinking for a moment, then ran to the bathroom and came out with his mum's toothbrush. He held it up and said with a charming little smile, "We better throw this one out too then, 'cause it fell in the toilet a few days ago."

At Sunday School they were teaching how God created everything, including human beings. A young boy seemed especially intent when they told him how Eve was created out of one of Adam's ribs.

Later in the week his mother noticed him lying down as though he were ill, and said, "What is the matter?"

The boy responded, "I have a pain in my side. I think I'm going to have a wife."

During the minister's prayer one Sunday, there was a loud whistle from one of the back pews. Gary's mother was horrified. She pinched him into silence, and after church, asked: "Gary, whatever made you do such a thing?" Gary answered soberly: "I asked God to teach me to whistle... And He just did!"

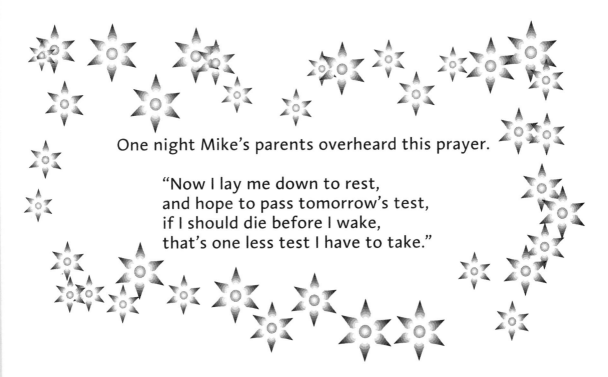

One night Mike's parents overheard this prayer.

"Now I lay me down to rest,
and hope to pass tomorrow's test,
if I should die before I wake,
that's one less test I have to take."

A five-year-old said grace at family dinner one night. "Dear God, thank you for these pancakes." When he concluded, his parents asked him why he thanked God for the pancakes when they were having chicken. He smiled and said, "I thought I'd see if He was paying attention tonight."

A rabbi said to a precocious six-year-old boy: "So your mother says your prayers for you each night? Very commendable. What does she say?" The little boy replied, "Thank God he's in bed!"

One Sunday a young boy was "acting up" during a church service. The parents did their best to maintain some sense of order in the pew but were losing the battle.

Finally the father picked the boy up and walked sternly down the aisle on his way out. Just before reaching the safety of the foyer the boy called loudly to the congregation, "Pray for me! Pray for me!"

The children were lined up in the cafeteria of a Catholic school for lunch. At the head of the table was a large pile of apples. The nun made a note, and posted it on the apple tray, "Take only one. God is watching."

Moving further along the lunch line, at the other end of the table was a large pile of chocolate chip cookies. One child whispered to another, "Take all you want. God is watching the apples."

When a woman found out she was pregnant, her four-year-old son overheard some of her private conversations with his dad. When a family friend asked the little boy if he was excited about the new baby, he replied,

"Yes! And I know what we're going to name it, too.

If it's a girl we're going to call her Grace, and if it's another boy we're going to call it quits!"

A two-year-old girl was with her mother while her older sister was at the dentist. She kept herself busy playing with toys in the waiting room until she noticed that her mum was resting, her eyes closed. With about six other patients in the waiting room, she marched up to her mother, looked at her and shook her shoulder. "Mummy," she yelled. "Wake up! This is not church!"

Christmas

The TOP SEVEN things overheard on the Wise Men's journey to Bethlehem:

7. Man, I'm starting to get a rush from this frankincense!
6. You guys ever eat camel meat? I hear it tastes like goat.
5. You know, I used to go to school with a girl named Beth Lehem.
4. What kind of name is Balthazar anyhow? Phoenician?
3. Hey, do either of you know why "MYRRH" is spelled with a "Y" instead of a "U"?
2. Okay, whose camel just spat?

And the NUMBER ONE thing overheard on the Wise Men's journey to Bethlehem…

1. All this staring at a star while riding a camel is making me woozy.

Christmas is a season of joy and good will, of singing and merriment and of generosity. Christmas is a season of sharing and love. Christmas is a season of concern for the needs of others, a season of the helping hand. And that's as it should be. For there is great satisfaction in making others happy.

Salvation Army, *The War Cry*

As a little girl climbed onto Santa's lap, Santa asked the usual, "And what would you like for Christmas?"

The child stared at him open mouthed and horrified for a minute, then gasped: "Didn't you get my e-mail?"

The three stages of a man's life:

1. He believes in Santa Claus;
2. He doesn't believe in Santa Claus;
3. He is Santa Claus.

It was Christmas and the judge was in a merry mood as he asked the prisoner, "What are you charged with?"

"Doing my Christmas shopping early," replied the defendant.

"That's no offence," said the judge. "How early were you doing this shopping?"

"Before the store opened," answered the defendant.

"The hinge of history is to be found on the door of a Bethlehem stable."

J. John

"Who but God goes up to heaven and comes back down? Who holds the wind in his fists? Who wraps up the oceans in his cloak? Who has created the whole wide world? What is his name and his son's name? Tell me if you can."

The Bible, Proverbs 30:4

One night Freda went carol singing.

She knocked on the door of a house and began to sing. A man with a violin in his hand came to the door.

Within half a minute tears were streaming down his face! Freda went on singing for half an hour, every carol she knew – and some she didn't.

As last she stopped.

"I understand," she said softly. "You are remembering your happy childhood Christmas days. You're a sentimentalist!"

"No," he sniffed. "I'm a musician!"

Clergy

Definition of clergy: those members of a community with high standards and low salaries.

It is considered that not enough training is given to clergy to prepare them for dealing with secretarial staff and it is hoped that the following points will assist them:

- ALWAYS remember that secretaries do not require to eat regularly. They therefore appreciate being given urgent tasks at lunchtime to be completed by first thing in the afternoon. To make them completely happy this work should be accompanied by the phrase: "I'm off for a quick lunch. I'll have that as soon as I get back."

- SECRETARIES do not have happy lives outside the office. You will therefore be extremely popular if you can delay your urgent work until the evening when the secretary is due to leave, thus ensuring that she does not have to spend long hours with her husband and family. She will especially enjoy preparing papers on morale and management.

- IF a secretary is obviously employed on an urgent task for another member of clergy, i.e. compiling important papers, she will appreciate your breaking her concentration with important questions like, "Why is there no soap in the toilet?" or "Have you seen my pencil?"

- IF, on entering your office, your secretary is engaged in conversation with a second person of equal or inferior status than yourself, then ignore the second person and speak directly to your secretary. If she appears not to hear, or her attention is wavering, then speak in a louder voice until you have her complete attention. An expert will develop this until they can stand 20 feet away from their secretary and shout down every other conversation in the room.

- THE procedure in the paragraph above is more effective if the secretary is talking on the telephone. She will enjoy the mental stimulation of trying to listen to the caller whilst you shout in her free ear.

- TO ensure your work is dealt with promptly and not overlooked, always place it in the centre of your secretary's desk. This is very important if she is already working on other papers at the time.

- WHEN amending drafts, ensure that amendments are written in faint pencil. Deletions, additions, arrows, balloons and writing in the margin will also help the secretary. Under no circumstances write in a legible manner.

- WP speed will also be improved if you appear at the secretary's desk every two minutes or so to ask how it is going.

- SECRETARIES have computer-like memories which they like to keep in training. It is sufficient

therefore to say: "There was a letter six months ago, I'm not sure of the subject, but I think I mentioned it – let me have a copy of it straight away."

- BE assured that if you follow these simple rules, your name will be passed from secretary to secretary throughout the parish, throughout the Church of England and your reputation will be firmly established.

- THE one sure way for clergy to impress their secretary is to redraft a letter or document five or more times and against a deadline. This shows the secretary that you are really intelligent, that you are considering all angles, that you are not put off by a more thorough marshalling of thoughts but are always open to the inspirational flash and have a father with a financial interest in a paper mill.

Commandments

> *A student was asked to list the Ten Commandments in any order. His answer? "3, 6, 1, 8, 4, 5, 9, 2, 10, 7."*

A woman was mailing an old family Bible to her brother in another part of the country.

"Is there anything breakable in here?" asked the postal clerk. "Only the Ten Commandments," answered the woman.

1. *Thou no gods shalt have but me*
2. *Before no idol bow the knee*
3. *Take not the name of God in vain*
4. *Dare not the Sabbath Day profane*
5. *Give to thy parents honour due*
6. *Take heed that thou no murder do*
7. *Abstain from words and deeds unclean*
8. *Steal not, for thou by God art seen*
9. *Tell no wilful lie and love it*
10. *What is thy neighbour's do not covet*

Commitment

> *"A nun should be, by the very nature of her vocation, a specialist in prayer. Or, to give it a more modern twist, she is a career woman in the field of prayer and contemplation."*
>
> **Mother Catherine Thomas**

A young man was a slow worker and found it difficult to hold down a job. After a visit to the employment office, he was offered work at the local zoo. When he arrived for his first day, the keeper, aware of his reputation, told him to take care of the tortoise section.

Later, the keeper dropped by to see how the young man was doing and found him standing by an empty enclosure with the gate open.

"Where are the tortoises?" he asked.

"I can't believe it," said the new employee, "I just opened the door and whooooosh, they were gone!"

Communication

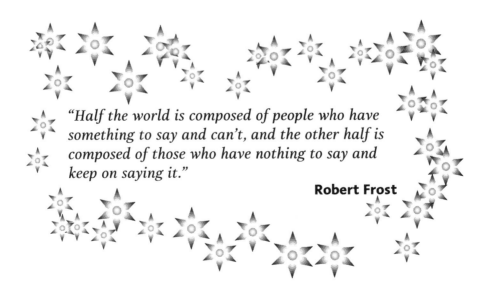

"Half the world is composed of people who have something to say and can't, and the other half is composed of those who have nothing to say and keep on saying it."

Robert Frost

A man takes his Rottweiler to the vet. "My dog's cross-eyed, is there anything you can do for him?"

"Well," says the vet, "let's have a look at him." So he picks the dog up and examines his eyes, then checks his teeth. Finally he says "I'm going to have to put him down."

"What? Because he's cross-eyed?"

"No, because he's really heavy."

The greatest problem in communication is the illusion that it has been accomplished.
Daniel W Davenport

To communicate is risky, not to communicate is riskier.

A husband and his wife were having some disagreements and were giving each other the silent treatment. The next day, the man realised that he would need his wife to wake him at 5:00am for an early morning business flight.

Not wanting to be the first to break the silence (AND LOSE), he wrote on a piece of paper, "Please wake me at 5:00am."

The next morning the man woke up, only to discover it was 7:00am and that he had missed his flight. Furious, he was about to go and see why his wife hadn't woken him when he noticed a piece of paper by the bed.

The paper said, "It is 5:00am. Wake up."

Some people leave without saying goodbye. Others say goodbye but take forever to leave.

A local priest and rabbi were fishing by the side of the road. After some discussion they thoughtfully made a sign saying, "The End is Near! Turn yourself around now before it's too late!" and showed it to each passing car.

One driver that drove by didn't appreciate the sign and shouted at them: "Leave us alone, you religious nuts!"

Shortly afterwards they heard a big splash. They looked at each other and the priest said to the rabbi, "You think we should just put up a sign that says 'Bridge Out' instead?"

"Discussion is an exchange of knowledge; argument is an exchange of ignorance."
Robert Wuiller

Some people don't have much to say and that's OK. But you have to listen to them a long time to find out.

"The volume of the average conversation could be enormously improved by the constant use of four simple words: 'I do not know'."
André Maurois

Communion

During the "children's sermon", the minister was talking about Communion and what it is all about.

"The Bible talks of Holy Communion being a 'joyful feast'. What does that mean? Well, 'joyful' means happy, right? And a feast is a meal. So a 'joyful feast' is a happy meal. He paused. And what are the three things we need for a happy meal?"

A little boy put up his hand and said, "Hamburger, fries, and a regular soft drink?"

Computers

A group of young children were sitting in a circle with their teacher. She was going round in turn asking them all questions.

"Peter, what noise does a cow make?"

"Moo"

"Anna, what noise does a cat make?"

"Meow"

"Jamie, what sound does a lamb make?"

"Baaa"

"Jenny, what sound does a mouse make?"

"Click"

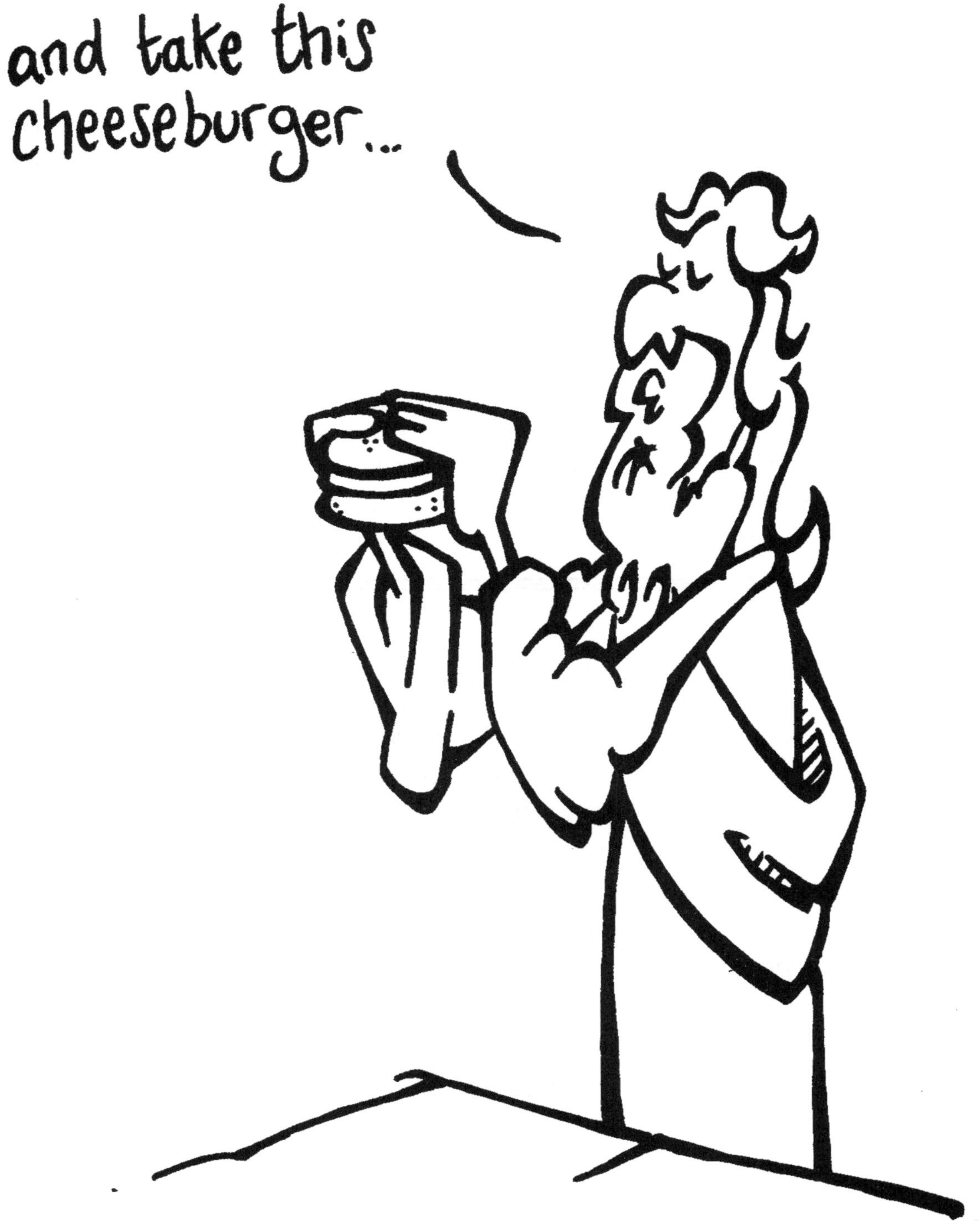
and take this cheeseburger...

There are three engineers in a car: an electrical engineer, a chemical engineer and a Microsoft engineer. Suddenly the car engine shuts off, leaving the three engineers stranded by the side of the road. All three engineers look at each other wondering what could be wrong. The electrical engineer suggests stripping down the electronics of the car and trying to trace where a fault might have occurred. The chemical engineer, not knowing much about cars, suggests that maybe the fuel is becoming emulsified and getting blocked somewhere. Then the Microsoft engineer, not knowing much about anything, comes up with a suggestion, "Why don't we close all the windows, get out, get back in, open the windows again, and maybe it'll work?"

The Lord is my programmer, I shall not crash.
He installed His software on the hard disk of my heart;
all of His commands are user-friendly.
His directory guides me to the right choices for His name's sake.
Even though I scroll through the problems of life,
I will fear no bugs, for He is my backup.
His password protects me.
He prepares a menu before me in the presence of my enemies.
His help is only a keystroke away.
Surely goodness and mercy will follow me all the days of my life,
and my file will be merged with His and saved forever.
Amen.

Courage

"Courage is what it takes to stand up and speak; courage is also what it takes to sit down and listen."
Winston Churchill

Don't be afraid to go out on a limb. That's where the fruit is.

It does not take a very brave dog to bark at the bones of a dead lion.

"The human spirit can endure a sick body, but who can bear it if the spirit is crushed?"
The Bible, Proverbs 18:14

"It was a bold man that first ate an oyster."
Jonathan Swift

An employee had been with a company for a year when he went in to ask for a raise.

"So soon?" said the boss, taken aback. "Certainly not. In this company you have to take time to work yourself up."

"I did," said the employee. "Look at me – I'm trembling all over."

Criticism

When criticised, try to remember an important truth from John Bunyan: "If my life is fruitless, it doesn't matter who praises me, and if my life is fruitful, it doesn't matter who criticises me."

Criticism, like rain, should be gentle enough to nourish one's growth without destroying one's roots.

Winston Churchill had the following words of Abraham Lincoln framed on the wall of his office:

"I do the very best I can. I mean to keep going. If the end brings me out all right, then what is said against me won't matter. If I'm wrong, ten angels swearing I was right won't make any difference."

A guest at a hotel restaurant called over the head waiter one morning and said, "I want two boiled eggs, one of them so undercooked that it's runny, the other so overcooked that it's about as easy to eat as rubber. Also grilled bacon that has been left on the plate to get cold, burnt toast that crumbles away as soon as you touch it with a knife, butter straight from the deep freeze that's impossible to spread, and a pot of very weak coffee, lukewarm."

"That's a complicated order, sir," said the bewildered waiter. "It might be a bit difficult."

"But that's exactly what you gave me yesterday."

"If you listen to constructive criticism you will be at home among the wise."
The Bible, Proverbs 15:31

Cross

Wellington represented the last formidable opposition to the French army under the command of Napoleon. Everything came to a head on the battlefield of Waterloo.

To communicate the outcome of the battle to English towns from Belgium, across the English Channel, a system of flashing lights was devised, which were to be emitted from one church top to another. When the battle ended, England had proved victorious and the message was sent, "Wellington Defeated Napoleon."

As the message was received and sent by each church towards the island of Great Britain, the fog began to rise. By the time the message reached the island, the fog cut the message short as the British churches received the message "Wellington Defeated." For hours, the nation feared the eventual overthrow of their country until the fog lifted and they had the complete message. "Wellington Defeated Napoleon."

On Good Friday, it looked as if the message was "Jesus Defeated." We must remember that that is not the complete message. When the fog lifted on Sunday, the rest of the message was revealed, "Jesus Defeated Death."

Don't believe in an incomplete message.

Culture

If biblical headlines were written by today's media:

On Red Sea crossing:
WETLANDS TRAMPLED IN LABOUR STRIKE
Pursuing Environmentalists Killed

On David vs. Goliath:
HATE CRIME KILLS BELOVED CHAMPION
Psychologist Questions Influence of Rock

On Elijah on Mount Carmel:
FIRE SENDS RELIGIOUS RIGHT EXTREMIST INTO FRENZY
400 Killed

On the birth of Christ:
HOTELS FULL, ANIMALS LEFT HOMELESS
Animal Rights Activists Enraged by Insensitive Couple

On feeding the 5,000:
PREACHER STEALS CHILD'S LUNCH
Disciples Mystified Over Behaviour

On healing the ten lepers:
LOCAL DOCTOR'S PRACTICE RUINED
"Faith Healer" Causes Bankruptcy

On healing of the Gadarene demoniac:
MADMAN'S FRIEND CAUSES STAMPEDE
Local Farmer's Investment Lost

On raising Lazarus from the dead:
FUNDAMENTALIST PREACHER RAISES A STINK
Will Reading to be Delayed

"The only difference between California and yoghurt is that yoghurt has attractive culture."
Woody Allen

"Knowledge of another culture should sharpen our ability to scrutinise more steadily, to appreciate more lovingly, our own."
Margaret Mead

D

Dangers

According to a report in October 2001, life has become more dangerous in the home.

Thirty-seven people hurt themselves using teapot warmers in 1999, compared with just 20 in 1998.

Trouser injuries also jumped, rising from 5,137 to 5,945 (victims included a 29-year-old woman who burned herself while ironing her trousers she was still wearing).

Hospital cases caused by socks and tights injuries rose by nearly 1,000 to 10,773.

Another 3,421 people nationwide were injured by clothes baskets, while 146 were hurt using bread bins. There were 329 toilet roll holder-related injuries.

Beanbag injuries climbed from 957 to 1,317 – making them four times as dangerous as meat cleavers.

The number of accidents involving tree trunks also rose, while mishaps with birdbaths soared from 117 to 311.

There was however some good news, with a drop in injuries inflicted by armchairs, which fell from 18,690 to 16,662.

Statistics compiled by the Home and Leisure Accident Surveillance System

Death

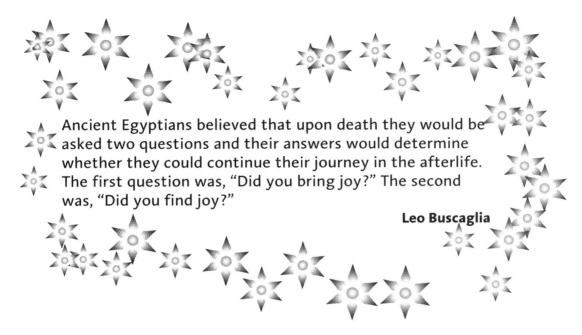

Ancient Egyptians believed that upon death they would be asked two questions and their answers would determine whether they could continue their journey in the afterlife. The first question was, "Did you bring joy?" The second was, "Did you find joy?"

Leo Buscaglia

A sick man turned to his doctor, as he was leaving the room after paying a visit, and said, "Doctor, I am afraid to die. Tell me what lies on the other side."

Very quietly the doctor said, "I don't know."

"You don't know? You, a Christian doctor, do not know what is on the other side?"

The doctor was holding the handle of the door, on the other side of which came a sound of scratching and whining, and as he opened the door a dog sprang into the room and leaped on him with an eager show of gladness. Turning to the patient, the doctor said,

"Did you notice my dog? He's never been in this room before. He didn't know what was inside. He knew nothing except that his master was here, and when the door opened he sprang in without fear. I know little of what is on the other side of death, but I do know one thing: I know my Master is there, and that is enough. And when the door opens, I shall pass through with no fear, but with gladness."

An exasperated mother, whose son was always getting into mischief, finally asked him, "How do you expect to get into Heaven?"

The boy thought it over and said, "Well, I'll just run in and out and in and out and keep slamming the door until St Peter says, 'For Heaven's sake, Jimmy, come in or stay out!'"

An ancient story is told about a slave who travelled with his master to Baghdad. As he walked the busy streets he found himself in the market place where he saw Death in human form. Death looked at him with such a piercing look that it frightened the slave, and he interpreted that look to mean that Death was planning soon to take his life.

He quickly rushed back to his master and told him what he had seen in the market place and asked if he might ride his camel to Samara, fifteen hours away, because he was sure that he would be safe there, for Death would not know where to find him. The master gave him permission, and quickly the slave was on his way to Samara.

A few hours later the master was in the market place where he also saw Death in human form. He walked up to Death and asked, "Why did you look at my slave with such a threatening look?" Death answered, "That was not a threatening look. That was a look of surprise. I had a date with him tonight in Samara and I was surprised to see him here in Baghdad."

I am ready to meet my Maker. Whether my Maker is prepared for the great ordeal of meeting me is another matter.
Winston Churchill

"Life is a great sunrise. I do not see why death should not be an even greater one."
Vladimir Nobokov

As men, we are all equal in the presence of death.
Publilius Syrus

When you were born, you cried and the world rejoiced. Live your life in a manner so that when you die the world cries and you rejoice.
Native American proverb

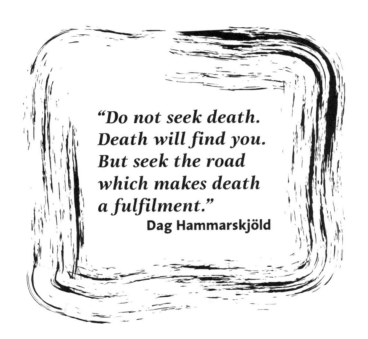

"Do not seek death. Death will find you. But seek the road which makes death a fulfilment."
Dag Hammarskjöld

A gang of eight-year-old boys found a dead bird. Feeling that a proper burial should be performed, they secured a small box, then dug a hole and made ready for the disposal of the deceased. The minister's son was chosen to say the appropriate prayers and with dignity intoned his version of what he thought his father always said,

"Glory be unto the Faaaather, and unto the Sonnnn…and into the hole you goooo."

Last WORDS

Inventor: Thomas Edison (1847–1931)
Oh my, it's very beautiful over there.

French Scientist: Pierre Simon Marquis de Laplace (1749–1827)
What we know is not much; what we do not know is immense.

Physicist: Sir Isaac Newton (1642–1727)
I do not know what I seem to the world, but to myself I appear to have been like a boy playing upon the seashore and diverting myself and then finding a smoother pebble or prettier shell than ordinary, while the great ocean of truth lay before me all undiscovered.

Diet

How to live longer:

The Japanese eat very little fat and suffer fewer heart attacks than the British or Americans.

The French eat a lot of fat and also suffer fewer heart attacks than the British or Americans.

The Japanese drink very little red wine and suffer fewer heart attacks than the British or Americans.

The Italians drink excessive amounts of red wine and suffer fewer heart attacks than the British or Americans.

The Germans drink a lot of beer and eat lots of sausages and fats and suffer fewer heart attacks than the British or Americans.

Conclusion: eat and drink what you like.

Speaking English is what kills you!

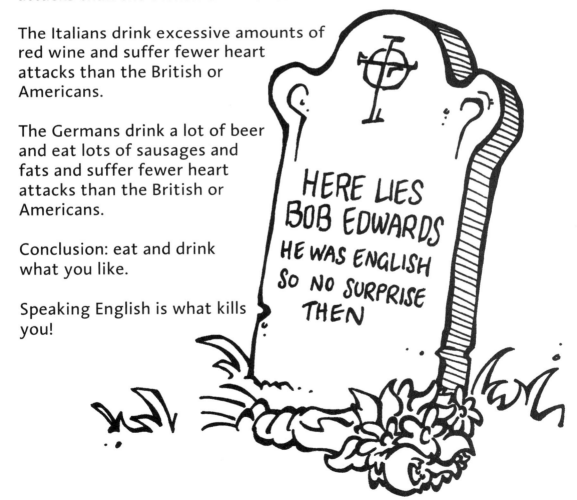

HERE LIES BOB EDWARDS HE WAS ENGLISH SO NO SURPRISE THEN

Direction

Robert Frost wrote, "Two roads diverged in a wood, and I took the one less travelled by, and that has made all the difference."
    What road are you on?

If at first you don't succeed, try reading the directions!

This present age seems more concerned about speed than direction.

If you don't know where you're going, any road will get you there.

The winds of God are always blowing,
but you must set the sails.

"It is comforting to know that not only the steps but also the stops of a good person are ordered by the Lord."
George Müller

It isn't enough to make sure you're on the right track;
you must also make sure you're going in the right direction.

"Seek his will in all you do, and he will direct your paths."
The Bible, Proverbs 3:6

Discouragement

Don't be discouraged; it may be the last key in the bunch that opens the door.

"Let us not get tired of doing what is right, for after a while we will reap a harvest of blessing if we don't get discouraged and give up."

The Bible, Galatians 6:9

Don't discourage the other person's plans unless you have better ones.

Never let discouragement be carried into a new day.

"No, I do not become discouraged. You see, God has not called me to a ministry of success. He has called me to a ministry of mercy."

Mother Teresa

E

Easter

German theologian Jurgen Moltmann expresses in a single sentence the great span from Good Friday to Easter Day: "God weeps with us so that we may someday laugh with him."

> If the Christ who died had stopped at the cross,
> His work had been incomplete.
> If the Christ who was buried had stayed in the tomb,
> He had only known defeat,
> But the way of the cross never stops at the cross
> and the way of the tomb leads on
> To victorious grace in the heavenly place
> where the risen Lord has gone.
>
> **Annie Johnson Flint**

Education

A young boy once approached his father to ask,
    "Dad, why does the wind blow?"
    "I don't know, son."
    "Dad, where do the clouds come from?"
    "I'm not sure, son."
    "Dad, what makes a rainbow?"
    "No idea, son."
    "Dad, do you mind me asking you all these questions?"
    "Not at all, son. How else are you going to learn?"

Do you know the difference between education and experience? Education is when you read the fine print; experience is what you get when you don't.
Pete Seeger, folk singer

"The glory of the young is their strength; the grey hair of experience is the splendour of the old."
The Bible, Proverbs 20:29

Ten famous people who never graduated:

Andrew Carnegie, US industrialist and philanthropist
Charles Chaplin, British actor and film director
Noel Coward, British actor, playwright, and composer
Charles Dickens, British novelist
Thomas Edison, US inventor
Maxim Gorky, Russian writer
Claude Monet, French painter
Sean O'Casey, Irish playwright
Henry M Stanley, British explorer
Mark Twain, writer

Emotion

A group of motion-picture engineers classified the following as the ten most dramatic sounds in the movies: a baby's first cry; the blast of a siren; the thunder of breakers on rocks; the roar of a forest fire; a foghorn; the slow drip of water; the galloping of horses; the sound of a distant train whistle; the howl of a dog; the wedding march. And one of these sounds causes more emotional response and upheaval than any other, has the power to bring forth almost every human emotion: sadness, envy, regret, sorrow, tears, as well as supreme joy. It is the wedding march.

Oliver Cromwell, who took the British throne away from Charles I and established the Commonwealth, said to a friend, "Do not trust to the cheering, for those persons would shout as much if you and I were going to be hanged."

Encouragement

The Duke of Wellington, the British military leader who defeated Napoleon at Waterloo, was not an easy man to serve under. He was brilliant, demanding, and not one to shower his subordinates with compliments. Yet even Wellington realised that his methods left something to be desired. In his old age a young lady asked him what, if anything, he would do differently if he had his life to live over again. Wellington thought for a moment, then replied. "I'd give more praise," he said.

Flatter me, and I may not believe you. Criticise me, and I may not like you. Ignore me, and I may not forgive you. Encourage me, and I will not forget you.
William Arthur Ward

Eternity

W B Hinson, an influential minister, spoke from his own experience just before he died.

He said, "I remember a year ago when a doctor told me, 'You have an illness from which you won't recover.' I walked out to where I live five miles from Portland, Oregon, and I looked across at that mountain that I love. I looked at the river in which I rejoice, and I looked at the stately trees that are always God's own poetry to my soul. Then in the evening I looked up into the great sky where God was lighting His lamps, and I said,

'I may not see you many more times, but Mountain, I shall be alive when you are gone; and River, I shall be alive when you cease running toward the sea; and Stars, I shall be alive when you have fallen from your sockets in the great down-pulling of the material universe!'"

Evil

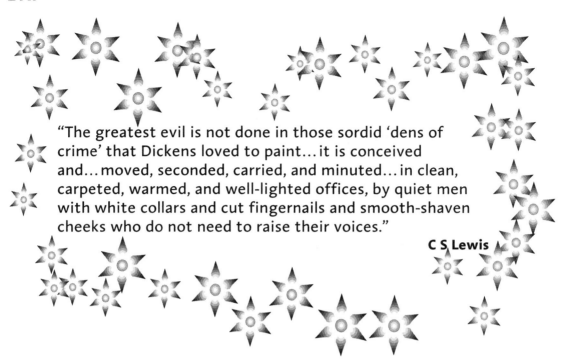

"The greatest evil is not done in those sordid 'dens of crime' that Dickens loved to paint…it is conceived and…moved, seconded, carried, and minuted…in clean, carpeted, warmed, and well-lighted offices, by quiet men with white collars and cut fingernails and smooth-shaven cheeks who do not need to raise their voices."

C S Lewis

Exercise

After dinner, rest a while.
After supper, walk a mile!

About the only part of the body that is over-exercised is the human jaw.

Some people pay someone to mow their lawns so they can play golf for exercise.

If you must exercise, why not exercise kindness?

"Most of the evils of life arise from our inability to sit still in a room."

Blaise Pascal

Jumping to conclusions is about the only exercise some people get!

"If it weren't for the fact that the TV set and the refrigerator are so far apart, some of us wouldn't get any exercise at all."

Joey Adams

Experience

Experience comes from what we have done. Wisdom comes from what we have done badly.

**Theodore Levitt,
Harvard Business School**

Experience is not what happens to you, it is what you do with what happens to you.
Aldous Huxley

Two friends are sitting in a pub watching the eleven o'clock news. A report comes on about a man threatening to jump from the 20th floor of a building. One friend turns to the other and says,

"I'll bet you £10 the guy doesn't jump."

"It's a bet," agrees his friend.

A few minutes later, the man on the ledge jumps, so the loser hands his pal a £10 note.

"I can't take your money," his friend admits. "I saw him jump earlier on the six o'clock news."

"Me, too," said the other friend. "But I didn't think he'd do it again!"

Faith

Feed your faith, and your doubts will starve to death.

"The world says, 'I'll believe it when I see it.' The Christian says, 'I'll see it when I believe it.'"

Mark Stibbe

"Faith is the art of holding on to things your reason has once accepted, in spite of your changing moods."

C S Lewis

"Faith is to believe what you do not see; the reward of faith is to see what you believe."

St Augustine

When we do what we can, God will do what we can't.

"God doesn't believe in atheists."

J. John

Faithfulness

When Adam stayed out very late for a few nights, Eve became upset. "You're running around with other women," she charged.

"You're being unreasonable," Adam responded. "You're the only woman on earth."

The quarrel continued until Adam fell asleep, only to be awakened by someone poking him in the chest. It was Eve.

"What do you think you're doing?" Adam demanded.

"Counting your ribs," said Eve.

Fathers

The Spanish have a story about a father and son who became estranged.

The son left home, and the father later set out to find him. He searched for months with no success.

Finally, in desperation, the father turned to the newspaper for help. His ad simply read, "Dear Paco, meet me in front of this newspaper office at noon on Saturday. All is forgiven. I love you. Your father."

On Saturday, 800 young men named Paco showed up looking for forgiveness and love from their estranged fathers.

After tucking their three-year-old child, Sam, in for bed one night, his parents heard sobbing coming from his room. Rushing back in, they found him crying hysterically. He told them that he had swallowed a penny and he was sure he was going to die. No amount of talking helped.

His father, in an attempt to calm him down, palmed a penny from his pocket and pretended to pull it from Sam's ear. Sam was delighted.

He snatched it from his father's hand, swallowed it, then cheerfully demanded, "Do it again, Dad!"

There is a story of Boswell, the famous biographer of Samuel Johnson. In his advanced years, Boswell reflected on the most important day of his life. He said it occurred one day during his youth, when his father had invited him to go fishing. While most of his childhood days had long since been forgotten, during that one day Boswell said that he learned about what life was about through example. Some industrious historian decided to track down the diary of Boswell's father to see how he reflected on that most important day in the life of his famous son. The entry: "Went fishing today with my son. A whole day wasted."

A teacher in New York decided to honour each of her Seniors in high school by telling them the difference they each made. She called each student to the front of the class, one at a time. First she told each of them how they had made a difference to her and the class. Then she presented each of them with a blue ribbon imprinted with gold letters, which read, "Who I Am Makes a Difference". Afterwards the teacher decided to do a class project to see what kind of impact recognition would have on a community. She gave each of the students three more ribbons and instructed them to go out and spread this acknowledgement ceremony. Then they were to follow up on the results, see who honoured whom and report back to the class in about a week.

One of the boys in the class went to a junior executive in a nearby company and honoured him for helping him with his career planning. He gave him a blue ribbon and put it on his shirt. Then he gave him two extra ribbons and said, "We're doing a class project on recognition, and we'd like you to go out, find somebody to honour, give them a blue ribbon, then give them the extra blue ribbon so they can acknowledge a third person to keep this acknowledgement ceremony going. Then please report back to me and tell me what happened." Later that day the junior executive went in to see his boss, who had been noted, by the way, as being kind of a grouchy fellow. He sat his boss down and he told him that he deeply admired him for being a creative genius. The boss seemed very surprised. The junior executive asked him if he would accept the gift of the blue ribbon and would he give him permission to put it on him. His surprised boss said, "Well, sure." The junior executive took the blue ribbon and placed it right on his boss's jacket above his heart. As he gave him the last extra ribbon, he said, "Would you do me a favour? Would you take this extra one and pass it on by honouring somebody else. The young boy who first gave me the ribbons is doing a project in school and we want to keep this recognition ceremony going and find out how it affects people."

That night the boss came home to his fourteen-year-old son and sat him down. He said, "The most incredible thing happened to me today. I was in my office and one of the junior executives came in and told me he admired me and gave me a blue ribbon for being a creative genius. Imagine. He thinks I'm a creative genius. Then he put this blue ribbon that says 'Who I Am Makes a Difference' on my jacket above my heart. He gave me an extra ribbon and asked me to find somebody else to honour. As I was driving home tonight, I started thinking about whom I would honour with this ribbon and I thought about you. I want to honour you. My days are really hectic and when I come home I don't pay a lot of attention to you. Sometimes I scream at you for not getting good enough grades in school and for your bedroom being a mess, but somehow tonight, I just wanted to sit here and, well, just let you know that you do make a difference to me. Besides your mother, you are the most important person in my life. You're a great kid and I love you!"

The startled boy started to sob and sob, and he wouldn't stop crying. His whole body shook. He looked up at his father and said through his tears, "Dad, earlier tonight I sat in my room and wrote a letter to you and Mom explaining why I had killed myself and asking you to forgive me. I was going to commit suicide tonight after you were asleep. I just didn't think that you cared at all. The letter is upstairs. I don't think I need it after all."

A boy at university wrote to his father, "I can't understand how you can call yourself a kind parent when you haven't sent me a cheque in two months! What kind of kindness is that?"

The father replied, "Son, that's called 'unremitting' kindness."

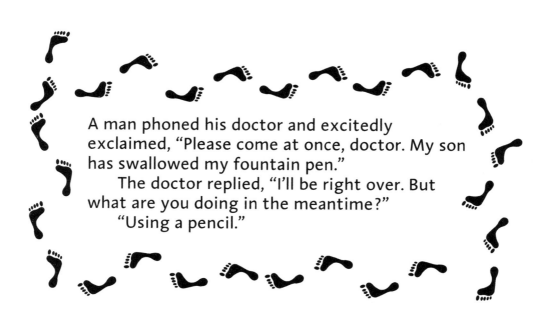

A man phoned his doctor and excitedly exclaimed, "Please come at once, doctor. My son has swallowed my fountain pen."

The doctor replied, "I'll be right over. But what are you doing in the meantime?"

"Using a pencil."

A young boy who had just got his driving licence asked his father, who was a minister, if they could discuss the use of the car. His father took him to his study and said to him, "I'll make a deal with you. You bring your grades up, study your Bible a little and get your hair cut and we'll talk about it."

After about a month the boy came back and again asked his father if they could discuss use of the car. They again went to the father's study where his father said,

"Son, I've been real proud of you. You have brought your grades up, you've studied your Bible diligently, but you didn't get your hair cut!"

The young man waited a moment and replied, "You know Dad, I've been thinking about that. You know, Samson had long hair, Moses had long hair, Noah had long hair, and even Jesus had long hair…"

To which his father replied, "Yes, and they walked everywhere they went!"

The new father, beside himself with excitement over the birth of his son, was determined to follow all the rules to the letter. "So, tell me, nurse," he said. "What time should we wake the little guy in the morning?"

Flying

A photographer for a national magazine was assigned to take pictures of a raging forest fire. He was told that at the local airport a small plane would be waiting to take him up.

He got to the airstrip just before sundown, and sure enough, there was a small Cessna waiting. He jumped in with his equipment and shouted, "Let's go!" The man sitting in the pilot's seat swung the plane into the wind, and soon they were flying erratically through the air.

"Fly over the north side of the fire," said the photographer, "and make several low-level passes."

"Why?" asked the pilot.

"Because I'm going to take pictures!" yelled the photographer. "That's what photographers do!"

The pilot replied, "You mean – you're not the flight instructor…?"

Folly

"It is better to be thought a fool than to open one's mouth and remove all doubt."
Mark Twain

"The wise look ahead to see what is coming, but fools deceive themselves."
The Bible, Proverbs 14:8

Forgiveness

The scene is a recent courtroom trial in South Africa:

A frail black woman rises slowly to her feet. She is something over 70 years of age. Facing across the room are several white security police officers, one of whom, Mr van der Broek, has just been tried and found implicated in the murders of both the woman's son and her husband some years before. He had come to the woman's home, taken her son, shot him at point blank range and then set the young man's body on fire while he and his officers partied nearby.

Several years later, van der Broek and his cohorts had returned to take away her husband as well. For many months she heard nothing of his whereabouts. Then almost two years after her husband's disappearance, van der Broek came back to fetch the woman herself. How vividly she remembers that evening, going to a place beside a river where she was shown her husband, bound and beaten, but still strong in spirit, lying on a pile of wood. The last words she heard from his lips as the officers poured gasoline over his body and set him aflame were, "Father forgive them…"

Now the woman stands in the courtroom and listens to the confessions offered by Mr van der Broek. A member of the South Africa's Truth and Reconciliation Commission turns to her and asks, "So what do you want? How should justice be done to this man who has so brutally destroyed your family?"

"I want three things," begins the old woman calmly, but confidently. "I want first to be taken to the place where my husband's body was burned so that I can gather up the dust and give his remains a decent burial."

She pauses, then continues. "My husband and son were my only family, I want secondly, therefore, for Mr van der Broek to become my son. I would like for him to come twice a month to the ghetto and spend a day with me so that I can pour out on him whatever love I still have remaining in me.

"And finally," she says, "I want a third thing. This is also the wish of my husband. And so, I would kindly ask someone to come to my side and lead me across the courtroom so that I can take Mr van der Broek in my arms and embrace him and let him know that he is truly forgiven." As the court assistants come to lead the elderly woman across the room, Mr van der Broek, overwhelmed by what he has just heard, faints. As he does, those in the courtroom, family, friends, neighbours – all victims of decades of oppression and injustice – begin to sing, softly but assuredly. "Amazing grace, how sweet the sound, that saved a wretch like me."

Freedom

"People demand freedom of speech to make up for the freedom of thought which they avoid."

Søren Kierkegaard

"Freedom is not primarily constituted of privileges but of responsibilities."

Albert Camus

"Some people's idea of free speech is that they are free to say what they like, but if anyone says anything back, that is an outrage."

Winston Churchill

"The truth shall set you free."
Jesus Christ

"Better to starve free than be a fat slave."

Aesop

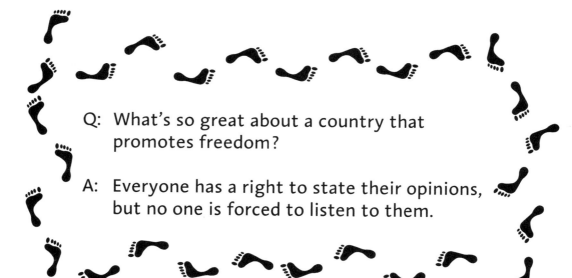

Q: What's so great about a country that promotes freedom?

A: Everyone has a right to state their opinions, but no one is forced to listen to them.

Future

An elderly carpenter was ready to retire. He told his employer-contractor of his plans to leave the house-building business and live a more leisurely life with his wife, enjoying his extended family. He would miss the pay cheque, but he needed to retire. They could get by.

The contractor was sorry to see his good worker go and asked if he could build just one more house as a personal favour. The carpenter said yes, but in time it was easy to see that his heart was not in his work. He resorted to shoddy workmanship and used inferior materials. It was an unfortunate way to end his career.

When the carpenter finished his work and his employer came to inspect the house, the contractor handed the front-door key to the carpenter. "This is your house," he said, "my gift to you."

What a shock! What a shame! If he had only known he was building his own house, he would have done it all so differently. Now he had to live in the home he had built none too well.

So it is with us. We build our lives in a distracted way, reacting rather than acting, willing to put up less than the best. At important points we do not give the job our best effort. Then with a shock we look at the situation we have created and find that we are now living in the house we have built. If we had realised that we would have done it differently.

Think of yourself as the carpenter. Think about your house. Each day you hammer a nail, place a board, or erect a wall. Build wisely. It is the only life you will ever build. Even if you live it for only one day more, that day deserves to be lived graciously and with dignity.

Your life tomorrow will be the result of your attitudes and the choices you make today.

G

Giving

A rejected opportunity to give is a missed opportunity to receive.

A four-year-old was in church when the wine and communion wafers were passed out. He was very interested in this, and started to get up. His mother leaned over and told him that he was not old enough to partake in the Communion.

Later, when the collection plate came by, he ignored it. His mother again leaned over and tried to coax some money out of him. He steadfastly refused, stating, "If I can't eat, I'm not paying."

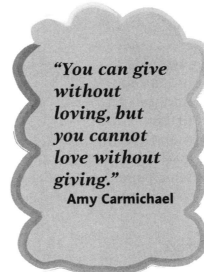

"You can give without loving, but you cannot love without giving."
Amy Carmichael

A well-worn dollar note and a similarly distressed $100 note arrived at the Bureau of Engraving and Printing to be retired. As they moved along the conveyor belt to the shredder they struck up a conversation. The $100 reminisced about its travels all over the country.

"I've had a pretty good life," the $100 note proclaimed. "Why, I've been to Las Vegas and Atlantic City, the finest restaurants in New York, performances on Broadway, and even a cruise from Miami."

"Wow!" said the single. "You really have gotten around."

"So tell me," says the $100, "where have you been throughout your lifetime?"

"Oh, I've been to the Methodist Church, the Baptist Church, the Presbyterian Church, the Lutheran Church, the Catholic Church, the Orthodox Church, Assembly of God Church, the Brethren Church, the United Church of Christ…"

And the $100 bill says, "What's a church?"

One beautiful Sunday morning, a minister announced to his congregation:

"My friends, I have here in my hands three sermons…a £100 sermon that lasts five minutes, a £50 sermon that lasts fifteen minutes, and a £10 sermon that lasts a full hour. Now, we'll take the collection and see which one I'll deliver."

"Blessed are those who are generous."
The Bible, Proverbs 22:9

Some give their mite, some give with all their might, and some don't give who might.

The story is told of a nun who was sitting at her window when the post arrived. She opened a letter from home and out fell a crisp new £10 note. As she read the letter accompanying the money, her eye was caught by the sight of a poorly dressed man on the street below. Thinking the man was probably not very well off, she placed the money in an envelope upon which she wrote "Don't Despair" and tossed it out of the window. The man picked up the envelope, opened it, and looked up at her smiling and tipped his hat.

The next day there was a knock at the convent door. Opening it, she found the man from the previous day holding out a handful of cash to her.

"What's this? I don't understand," she said.

"Lady," he replied, "it's your cut. 'Don't Despair' paid five to one yesterday."

Henry Ford returned to his beloved Ireland, and part of his tour was to include the opening of a new hospital.

The fund raisers pointed out to Henry that they were £5,000 short of the total funds needed to complete the hospital.

Henry said: "I will give you £500 towards the shortfall."

The next day it was reported in the press on the front page: "Henry Ford the multimillionaire founder of the great Ford motor company has given £500 towards the outstanding sum of £5,000 required to complete the hospital."

Henry Ford was so embarrassed by this headline that he did a deal with the organisers. He said, "Look I will give you all the money on two conditions: one, that it is reported that the correspondent made a mistake and that I actually gave the full £5,000 outstanding; and two, that you put over the hospital door these words from the Scriptures: 'I came to you a stranger and you took me in'."

Grace

Setting: A small rural community, so small, in fact, that the minister of the only church in town must also double up as the local barber to make ends meet.

There happened to be a man in this small community who had invested wisely and was enjoying his newfound comfort. This man got out of bed one day to go through his daily routine. He looked into the mirror as he was about to shave and decided, "I make enough money now, I don't have to shave myself. I'll go down to the barber and let him shave me from now on." So he did.

He walked into the barber shop and found the minister/barber was out calling on the housebound. His wife, Grace, said "I usually do the shaves anyway – sit down and I'll shave you." So he did. She shaved him and he asked, "How much do I owe you?"

"$25," Grace replied. The man thought that was somewhat expensive and that he may have to get a shave every other day.

Nonetheless, he paid Grace and went on his way.

The next day, he woke up and found his face to be just as smooth as the day before. No need for a shave today, he thought, well, it was a $25 shave.

The next day he awoke to find his face as smooth as a baby's bottom. Wow! he thought. That's amazing. He normally would need to shave daily to keep his clean-shaven business look.

On the third day, he woke up and his face was still as smooth as the minute after Grace had finished. Now somewhat perplexed, the man went down to the barber shop to ask some questions.

This particular day the minister was in and the man asked him why his face was as smooth as it had been the first day it was shaven.

The kind old pastor gently retorted, "Friend, you were shaved by Grace…and once shaved, always shaved."

Grandchildren

The little boy greeted his grandmother with a hug and said, "I'm so happy to see you grandma! Now daddy will do the trick he has been promising us."

The grandmother was curious. "What trick is that, my dear?" she asked.

The little boy replied, "I heard daddy tell mummy that he would climb the walls if you came to visit us again."

When I stopped the bus to pick up Chris for nursery, I noticed an older woman hugging him as he left the house.

"Is that your grandmother?" I asked.

"Yes," Chris said. "She's come to visit us for Christmas."

"How nice," I said. "Where does she live?"

"At the airport," Chris replied. "Whenever we want her, we just go out there and get her."

I didn't know if my granddaughter had learned her colours yet, so I decided to test her. I would point out something and ask what colour it was. She would tell me, and she was always correct. But it was fun for me, so I continued. At last, she headed for the door, saying sadly,

"Grandma, I think you should try to figure out some of these yourself!"

When the grandmother returned from the supermarket, her small grandson pulled out the box of animal biscuits he had begged for, then he spread the animal-shaped biscuits all over the kitchen counter.

"What are you doing?" his grandmother asked.

"The box says you can't eat them if the seal is broken," the boy explained. "I'm looking for the seal."

In the supermarket was a man pushing a trolley that contained a screaming, bellowing baby. The gentleman kept repeating softly, "Don't get excited, Albert; don't scream, Albert; don't yell, Albert; keep calm, Albert."

A woman standing next to him said, "You certainly are to be commended for trying to soothe your grandson Albert."

The man looked at her and said, "Lady, I'm Albert."

While working for an organisation that delivers lunches to elderly housebound people, I used to take my four-year-old daughter on my afternoon rounds. She was unfailingly intrigued by the various appliances of old age, particularly the canes, walking frames and wheelchairs. One day I found her staring at a pair of false teeth soaking in a glass. As I braced myself for the inevitable barrage of questions, she merely turned and whispered, "The tooth fairy will never believe this!"

Gratitude

Today I stood at my window and cursed the pouring rain,
Today a desperate farmer prayed for his fields of grain
My weekend plans are ruined, it almost makes me cry
While the farmer lifts his arms and blesses the clouded sky.
The alarm went off on Monday and I cursed my work routine,
Next door a laid-off mechanic feels the empty pockets of his jeans.
I can't wait for my vacation, some time to take for me,
He doesn't know tonight how he'll feed his family.
I cursed my leaky roof and the grass I need to mow,
A homeless man downtown checks for change in the telephone.
I need a new car, mine is getting really old,
He huddles in a doorway, seeking shelter from the cold.
With blessings I'm surrounded, the rain, a job, a home,
Though my eyes are often blinded by the things I think I own.

"In everything
give thanks."
**The Bible,
1 Thessalonians 5:18**

"If you pick up a starving dog and make him prosperous, he will not bite you; that is the principal difference between a dog and a man."

Mark Twain

Two students were working their way through university. Their funds got desperately low and the idea came to them to engage Ignacy Paderewski for a piano recital. They would use the funds to pay their board and lodging.

The pianist's manager requested a guarantee of $2,000. The guarantee was a great deal of money, but the students agreed and proceeded to promote the concert. They worked hard and after paying for the publicity and the hall, they were left with only $1,600.

After the concert the two students told the great artist the bad news. They gave him the entire $1,600 along with an IOU for the remaining $400, explaining that they would earn the amount at the earliest possible opportunity and send the money to him. It looked like the end of their college careers.

"No," replied Paderewski. "That won't do." Then, tearing the note in two, he returned the money to them.

"Now," he told them, "take out of the $1,600 all you need and let me have the rest."

The years rolled by – World War 1 came and went. Paderewski, now premier of Poland, was striving to feed thousands of starving people in his native land. The only person in the world who could help him was Herbert Hoover, who was in charge of the US Food and Relief Bureau. Hoover responded and soon thousands of tons of food were sent to Poland.

After the starving people were fed, Paderewski journeyed to Paris to thank Hoover for the relief sent him.

"That's all right, Mr Paderewski," was Hoover's reply.

"Besides, you don't remember it, but you helped my friend and me once when I was a student at university and I was in trouble."

Hearing

An elderly gentleman had serious hearing problems for a number of years. He went to the doctor who fitted a set of hearing aids that allowed the gentleman to hear again.

The elderly gentleman returned to the doctor's in a month for a final check on the new equipment. After some tests, the doctor proclaimed, "Your hearing is perfect!"

"Thank you for helping me," replied the elderly man.

"You're welcome," said the doctor.

"Your family must be really pleased that you can hear again."

"Oh, I haven't told them yet. I just sit around and listen to the conversations I used to miss," replied the elderly gentleman.

"Really?" questioned the doctor. "You must still be marvelling at being able to hear again and just not ready to believe it yourself. That must be why you haven't told them."

"Well, no, that's not it exactly, but I have changed my will three times!"

Heaven

"If you read history you find that the Christians who did most for the present world were precisely those who thought most of the next."

C S Lewis

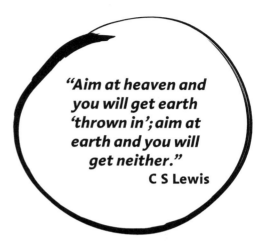

"Aim at heaven and you will get earth 'thrown in'; aim at earth and you will get neither."

C S Lewis

"Heaven: where questions and answers become one."

Elie Wiesel

Many years ago a man conned his way into the orchestra of the emperor of China although he could not play a note. Whenever the group practised or performed, he would hold his flute against his lips, pretending to play but not making a sound. He received a modest salary and enjoyed a comfortable living.

Then one day the emperor requested a solo from each musician. The flautist got nervous. There wasn't enough time to learn the instrument. He pretended to be sick, but the royal physician wasn't fooled. On the day of his solo performance, the impostor took poison and killed himself. The explanation of his suicide led to a phrase that found its way into the English language: "He refused to face the music."

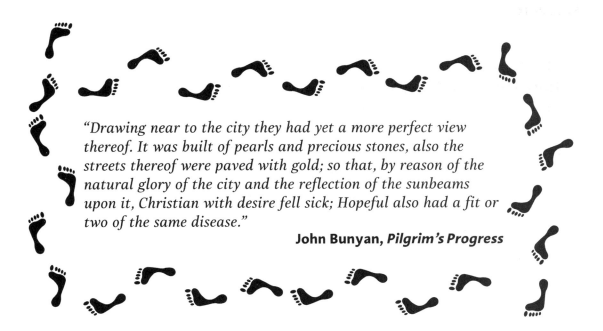

"Drawing near to the city they had yet a more perfect view thereof. It was built of pearls and precious stones, also the streets thereof were paved with gold; so that, by reason of the natural glory of the city and the reflection of the sunbeams upon it, Christian with desire fell sick; Hopeful also had a fit or two of the same disease."

John Bunyan, *Pilgrim's Progress*

"If I sold my house and my car, had a big garage sale and gave all my money to the church, would that get me into Heaven?" I asked the children in my Sunday School class.

"NO!" the children all answered.

"If I cleaned the church every day, mowed the grass, and kept everything neat and tidy, would that get me into Heaven?"

Again, the answer was, "NO!"

"Well, then, if I was kind to animals and gave candy to all the children, and loved my wife, would that get me into Heaven?" I asked them again.

Again, they all answered, "NO!"

"Well, I continued, "then how can I get into Heaven?"

A five-year-old boy shouted out, "YOU GOTTA BE DEAD!"

A Christian woman had to do a lot of travelling for her business. Flying made her nervous, so she always took her Bible along with her to read and it helped relax her.

One time, she was sitting next to a man. When he saw her pull out her Bible, he gave a little chuckle and went back to what he was doing. After a while, he turned to her and asked,

"You don't really believe all that stuff in there, do you?"

The woman replied, "Of course I do. It is the Bible."

He said, "Well, what about that guy that was swallowed by that whale?"

She replied, "Oh, Jonah. Yes, I believe that, it is in the Bible."

He asked, "Well, how do you suppose he survived all that time inside the whale?"

The woman said, "Well, I don't really know. I guess when I get to Heaven, I will ask him."

"What if he isn't in Heaven?" the man asked sarcastically.

"Then you can ask him," replied the woman.

The Pope dies and goes to Heaven. When he gets there, St Peter shows him to his new quarters which turn out to be a tiny one-bedroom apartment.

The Pope is horrified and wants to know why he doesn't have the penthouse apartment, which is huge.

St Peter informs him that the resident of the penthouse is a lawyer.

"A lawyer," says the Pope. "But I'm the Pope, surely I'm more important?"

"With respect, Sir," says St Peter, "We have lots of Popes up here, but we only have ONE lawyer!"

Husbands

A husband shopping centre was opened, where a woman could choose a husband from a wide selection of men.

It was laid out on five floors, with the men increasing in positive attributes as you ascended the floors. The only rules were that once you opened the door to any floor, you must choose a man from that floor. And if you went up a floor, you couldn't go back down, except to leave the place.

So, a couple of girlfriends go to the shopping centre to find a husband.

First floor: the door has a sign saying "These men have jobs and love kids." The women read the sign and say, "Well, that's better than not having jobs or not loving kids, but let's see what's further up."

And up they go.

Second floor: "These men have high paying jobs, love kids and are extremely good looking." "Hmmm," say the girls. "But, what's further up?"

Third floor: "These men have high paying jobs, are extremely good looking, love kids, and help with the housework."

"Wow!" say the women. "Very tempting, but there's more further up!"

And so again, up they go.

Fourth floor: "These men have high paying jobs, love kids, are extremely good looking, help with the housework and have a strong romantic streak."

"Oh, wow!" they exclaim. "But, just think what must be awaiting us further on!"

So, up to the fifth floor they go. The sign on the door says:

"This is just to prove that women are impossible to please. Thank you for shopping, and have a nice day."

> "Men are horribly tedious when they are good husbands, and abominably conceited when they are not."
>
> **Oscar Wilde**

> *"Husbands are like fires. They go out if unattended."*
>
> **Zsa Zsa Gabor**

A diplomatic husband said to his wife, "How do you expect me to remember your birthday when you never look any older?"

Hygiene

If you are a regular traveller on the London Underground, here are some facts which you are going to wish you hadn't read.

During the autumn of 2000, a team of scientists at the Department of Forensics at University College London removed a row of passenger seats from a Central Line tube carriage for analysis into cleanliness. Despite London Underground's claim that the interior of their trains are cleaned on a regular basis, the scientists made some alarming discoveries.

Much of it is unrepeatable. This is just the part we COULD publish.

When the seats were taken apart, they found:

- the remains of 6 mice and 2 rats
- one previously unheard of fungus

As a result of this research, it is estimated that by holding one of the armrests, you are transferring, to your body, the natural oils and sweat from as many as 400 different people.

It is estimated that it is generally healthier to smoke five cigarettes a day than to travel for one hour a day on the London Underground.

It is far more hygienic to wipe your hand on the inside of a recently flushed toilet bowl before eating, than to wipe your hand on a London Underground seat before eating.

It is estimated that, within London, more sick-days are taken because of bugs picked up whilst travelling on the London Underground than for any other reason (including alcohol).

Hymns

Hymns for Different Occupations:

DENTIST: Crown Him with many crowns

CONTRACTORS: The church's one foundation

OBSTETRICIANS: Come, labour on

GOLFERS: There is a green hill far away

POLITICIANS: Standing on the promises

LIBRARIANS: Let all mortal flesh keep silence

LAWYERS: In the hour of trial

DRY CLEANERS: O for a faith that will not shrink

CREDIT CARD USERS: A charge to keep have I

CENSUS TAKERS: All people that on earth do dwell

TAXATION OFFICERS: We give thee but thine own

TRAFFIC ENGINEERS: Where cross the crowded ways of life

I

Identity

In *The Mask Behind the Mask*, biographer Peter Evans says that actor Peter Sellers played so many roles he sometimes was not sure of his own identity. Approached once by a fan who asked him, "Are you Peter Sellers?" Sellers answered briskly, "Not today," and walked on.

The dilemma of an unclear sense of personal identity was illustrated by an incident in the life of the famous German philosopher Schleiermacher, who did much to shape the progress of modern thought. The story is told that one day, when an old man, he was sitting alone on a bench in a city park. A policeman thinking that he was a vagrant came over and shook him and asked, "Who are you?" Schleiermacher replied sadly, "I wish I knew."

Incarnation

"The most significant achievement of our age is not that man stood on the moon, but rather that God in Christ stood upon this earth."

The US astronaut, James Irwin, on his return to earth after standing on the moon

The mystery of the humanity of Christ, that He sunk Himself into our flesh, is beyond all human understanding.

Martin Luther, *Table Talk*

The Maker of man became man that He, Ruler of the stars, might be nourished at the breast; that He, the Bread, might be hungry; that He, the Fountain, might thirst; that He, the Light, might sleep; that He, the Way, might be wearied by the journey; that He, the Truth, might be accused by false witnesses; that He, the Judge of the living and the dead, might be brought to trial by a mortal judge; that He, Justice, might be condemned by the unjust; that He, Discipline, might be scourged with whips; that He, the Foundation, might be suspended upon a cross; that Courage might be weakened; that Security might be wounded; that Life might die.

St Augustine

He began His ministry by being hungry, yet He is the Bread of Life.
Jesus ended His earthly ministry by being thirsty, yet He is the Living Water.
Jesus was weary, yet He is our rest.
Jesus paid tribute, yet He is the King.
Jesus was accused of having a demon, yet He cast out demons.
Jesus wept, yet He wipes away our tears.
Jesus was sold for thirty pieces of silver, yet He redeemed the world.
Jesus was brought as a lamb to the slaughter, yet He is the Good Shepherd.
Jesus died, yet by His death He destroyed the power of death.

Gregory of Nazianzus, AD 381

British statesman and financier Cecil Rhodes, whose fortune was used to endow the world-famous Rhodes Scholarships, was a stickler for correct dress – but not at the expense of someone else's feelings.

A young man invited to dine with Rhodes arrived by train and had to go directly to Rhodes' home in his travel-stained clothes. Once there he was appalled to find the other guests already assembled, wearing full evening dress.

After what seemed a long time Rhodes appeared, in a shabby old blue suit. Later the young man learned that his host had been dressed in evening clothes, but put on the old suit when he heard of his young guest's dilemma.

Lying at your feet is your dog. Imagine, for the moment, that your dog and every dog is in deep distress. Some of us love dogs very much. If it would help all the dogs in the world to become like men, would you be willing to become a dog? Would you put down your human nature, leave your loved ones, your job, hobbies, your art and literature and music, and choose instead of the intimate communion with your beloved, the poor substitute of looking into the beloved's face and wagging your tail, unable to smile or speak? Christ by becoming man limited the thing which to Him was the most precious thing in the world; his unhampered, unhindered communion with the Father.

C S Lewis

Information

Inhumanity

The following true story, reported on Saturday 9 March 2002, takes the biscuit when it comes to inhumanity. The incident is made all the more appalling by virtue of the fact that the perpetrator was a member of a caring profession:

"A nurse has been arrested for murder after running over a tramp, driving home with him stuck headfirst through her windscreen, and then ignoring his pleas for help as he bled to death in her garage. Police said Gregory Biggs, 37, was trapped for up to three days on the front of the parked Chevrolet, his legs dangling across the bonnet, before he died from loss of blood. He would have lived had he received medical attention. Chante Mallard, 25, a nurse's aid from Fort Worth, Texas, said in her defence that she went out to check on him from time to time and apologised to him for his situation. She stopped short, however, of calling an ambulance… The Tarrant County District Attorney said, 'I am going to have to come up with a new word. Indifferent isn't enough. Cruel isn't enough. Heartless? Inhumane? Maybe we've just redefined inhumanity.'"

Initiative

Going to bed the other night I noticed people in my shed stealing things. I phoned the police but was told no one was in the area to help. They said they would send someone over as soon as possible.

I hung up. A minute later I rang again. "Hello," I said, "I called you a minute ago because there were people in my shed. You don't have to hurry now, because I've shot them."

Within minutes there were half a dozen police cars in the area, plus helicopters and an armed response unit. They caught the burglars red-handed.

One of the officers said: "I thought you said you'd shot them."

To which I replied: "I thought you said there was no one in the area."

Insight

Charles Steinmetz retired from General Electric after a lifelong career. Later, a system breakdown had GE engineers stumped, so they called on Steinmetz as a consultant. After inspecting the machinery at length, he marked an "X" on a defective part and billed GE for $10,000. The company protested, asking for an itemisation. Steinmetz's reply read simply:

Making one chalk mark: $1.00
Knowing where to place it: $9,999

Irony

English novelist William Golding tells with delight of the policewoman in a Wiltshire town near his home who gave him a parking ticket the day after he won the 1983 Nobel Prize in Literature. "Can't you read?" she demanded.

Announcement in the weekly journal *Planning*: "We are sorry that the Planning Directory has so far not appeared. This is because it is considerably bigger than originally anticipated and is taking longer to print."

J

Jesus

It has been said that Socrates and Aristotle each taught for 40 years, Plato for 50 years, but Jesus for only three. Yet His influence far surpasses the combined 130 years of teaching by these men who are acknowledged as the greatest philosophers of all antiquity. He painted no pictures, yet the finest paintings of Raphael, Michelangelo and Leonardo da Vinci received their illumination from Him. He wrote no poetry, yet Dante, Milton and others of the world's greatest poets were inspired by Him. He composed no music, yet Haydn, Handel, Beethoven and Bach reached their highest perfection in hymns, symphonies and oratorios composed in His honour. Jesus is quite simply the greatest teacher who ever lived.

In Jesus Christ we have:

A love that can never be fathomed
A life that can never die
A righteousness that can never be tarnished
A peace that can never be understood
A rest that can never be disturbed
A joy that can never be diminished
A hope that can never be disappointed
A glory that can never be clouded
A light that can never be darkened
A purity that can never be defiled
A beauty that can never be marred
A wisdom that can never be baffled
Resources that can never be exhausted.

Anon

Christ for sickness, Christ for health,
Christ for poverty, Christ for wealth,
Christ for joy, Christ for sorrow,
Christ today and Christ tomorrow;
Christ my Life, and Christ my Light,
Christ for morning, noon and night,
Christ when all around gives way
Christ my everlasting Stay;
Christ my Rest, and Christ my Food
Christ above my highest good,
Christ my Well-beloved Friend
Christ my Pleasure without end;
Christ my Saviour, Christ my Lord
Christ my Portion, Christ my God,
Christ my Shepherd, I His sheep
Christ Himself my soul to keep;
Christ my Leader, Christ my Peace
Christ hath wrought my soul's release,
Christ my Righteousness divine
Christ for me, for He is mine;
Christ my Wisdom, Christ my Meat,
Christ restores my wandering feet,
Christ my Advocate and Priest
Christ who ne'er forgets the least;
Christ my Teacher, Christ my Guide,
Christ my Rock, in Christ I hide,
Christ the Ever-living Bread,
Christ His precious Blood hath shed;
Christ hath brought me nigh to God,
Christ the everlasting Word
Christ my Master, Christ my Head,
Christ who for my sins hath bled;
Christ my Glory, Christ my Crown,
Christ the Plant of great renown,
Christ my Comforter on high,
Christ my Hope draws ever nigh.
Anon

Jesus Christ is the meeting place of eternity and time, the joining of deity and humanity, the junction of heaven and earth.

*"No other God have I but Thee;
Born in a manger, died on a tree."*
Martin Luther

"The name of Jesus is not so much written as ploughed into the history of the world."
Ralph Waldo Emerson

K

Kindness

"Kindness consists in loving people more than they deserve."
Joseph Joubert

If you're unkind, you're the wrong kind.

Kindness makes a person attractive. If you would win the world, melt it, do not hammer it.
Alexander Maclaren

"Never let loyalty and kindness get away from you! Wear them like a necklace; write them deep within your heart."
The Bible, Proverbs 3:3

Don't expect to enjoy the cream of life if you keep the milk of kindness bottled up.

"When I was young I admired clever people. Now that I'm old I admire kind people."
Abraham Heschel

"Constant kindness can accomplish much. As the sun makes ice melt, kindness causes misunderstandings, mistrust and hostility to evaporate."
Albert Schweitzer

"If you want to lift yourself up, lift up someone else."
Booker T Washington

Wherever there is a human being there is an opportunity for kindness.

Kindness pays more when you don't pay for it.

"No act of kindness, no matter how small, is ever wasted."
Aesop

A tourist ordered breakfast in a restaurant. The waitress was rather grumpy and rude, and when his breakfast arrived, he looked up at the waitress and asked, "How about a kind word?" She leaned over to him and said, "Don't eat the eggs!"

A man is in bed with his wife when there is a rat-a-tat-tat on the door. He rolls over and looks at his clock, and it's half past three in the morning.

"I'm not getting out of bed at this time," he thinks, and rolls over.

Then, a louder knock follows. "Aren't you going to answer that?" says his wife. So he drags himself out of bed and goes downstairs. He opens the door and there is a man standing at the door. It didn't take the homeowner long to realise the man was drunk. "Hi there," slurs the stranger, "Can you give me a push?"

"No, get lost. It's half past three. I was in bed," says the man and slams the door.

He goes back up to bed and tells his wife what happened.

She says, "Tom, that wasn't very nice of you. Remember that night we broke down in the pouring rain on the way to pick the kids up from the baby sitter and you had to knock on a stranger's door and ask for help? What would have happened if he'd told us to get lost?"

"But this guy is drunk," says the husband.

"It doesn't matter," says his wife. "He needs our help and it would be the Christian thing to help him."

So the husband gets out of bed again, gets dressed, and goes downstairs. He opens the door and not being able to see the stranger anywhere, he shouts, "Hey, do you still want a push?"

And he hears a voice cry out, "Yes, please."

So, still being unable to see the stranger, he shouts, "Where are you?"

The drunk replies, "Over here, on the swing."

Kissing

Some insurance companies and psychologists have found a correlation between work attitudes and a morning goodbye kiss. Studies show that men who do not kiss their wives goodbye are apt to be moody, depressed and disinterested in their jobs. But kissing husbands start off the day on a positive note. This positive attitude results in more efficient and safer driving practices. Kissing husbands live five years longer than their less romantic counterparts. However, kissing may be more a consequence than a cause of a happy life situation. The subject warrants continued investigation by every husband and wife.

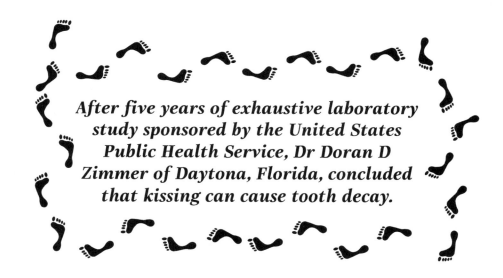

After five years of exhaustive laboratory study sponsored by the United States Public Health Service, Dr Doran D Zimmer of Daytona, Florida, concluded that kissing can cause tooth decay.

Before I heard the doctors tell the dangers of a kiss,
I had considered kissing you the nearest thing to bliss.
But now I know biology and sit and sigh and moan;
Six million mad bacteria, and I thought we were alone.

Anon

Knowledge

The sum total of man's knowledge could be represented graphically:

Up to 1845 = 1 inch
1845 to 1945 = 3 inches
1945 to 1976 = the height of the Washington Monument

For every man, education should be a process which continues all his life. We have to abandon, as swiftly as possible, the idea that schooling is something restricted to youth. How can it be, in a world where half the things a man knows at 20 are no longer true at 40 – and half the things he knows at 40 hadn't been discovered when he was 20?

Arthur C Clarke

Knowledge is exploding at such a rate – more than 2,000 pages a minute – that even Einstein couldn't keep up. In fact, if you read 24 hours a day, from age 21 to 70, and retained all you read, you would be one and a half million years behind when you finished.

Laughter

While the average child laughs 150 times a day, say researchers at the University of Michigan, the average adult laughs only 15 times.

In *The Anatomy of an Illness: As Perceived by the Patient*, Norman Cousins tells of being hospitalised with a rare, crippling disease. When he was diagnosed as incurable, Cousins checked out of the hospital. Aware of the harmful effects that negative emotions can have on the body, Cousins reasoned the reverse was true. So he borrowed a movie projector and prescribed his own treatment, consisting of Marx Brothers films and old *Candid Camera* reruns. It didn't take long for him to discover that ten minutes of laughter provided two hours of pain-free sleep. Amazingly, his debilitating disease was eventually reversed. After the account of his victory appeared in the *New England Journal of Medicine*, Cousins received more than 3,000 letters from appreciative physicians throughout the world.

Happy is the person who can laugh at himself. He will never cease to be amused.
Habib Bourguiba

"A glad heart makes a happy face."
The Bible, Proverbs 15:13

Leadership

Effective leaders concentrate on the things they are able to change; ineffective leaders spend their energy on things they are very unlikely ever to be able to change.

Anon

"A leader is a dealer in hope."
Napoleon Bonaparte

"The leader must know, must know that they know, and must be able to make it abundantly clear to others that they know."
Clarence Randall

We herd sheep;
we drive cattle;
we lead people.

In order to be a leader a man must have followers. And to have followers, a man must have their confidence. Hence the supreme quality of a leader is unquestionably integrity. Without it, no real success is possible, no matter whether it is on a section gang, on a football field, in an army, or in an office. If a man's associates find him guilty of phoniness, if they find that he lacks forthright integrity, he will fail. His teachings and actions must square with each other. The first great need, therefore, is integrity and high purpose.

Dwight D Eisenhower

Matthew Henry – a minister – met a young woman of the nobility, who was also wealthy, and they fell in love. She went to ask her father if she could marry him and he said, "He's got no background, you don't know where he's come from."

She said, "Yes, I know, but I know where he's going and I want to go with him."

A leader is a person with a magnet in his heart and a compass in his head.
Vance Hainer

John W Gardner, former Secretary of the US Department of Health, Education, and Welfare, who is now directing a leadership study project in Washington, DC, has pinpointed five characteristics that set "leader" managers apart from run-of-the-mill managers:

They are long-term thinkers who see beyond the day's crisis and the quarterly report.

Their interest in the company does not stop with the unit they are heading. They want to know how all of the company's departments affect one another, and they are constantly reaching beyond their specific area of influence.

They put heavy emphasis on vision, values, and motivation.

They have strong people skills.

They don't accept the status quo.

Do not follow where the path may lead, go instead where there is no path and leave a trail.

The trouble with being a leader today is that you can't be sure whether people are following you or chasing you.

Bruce Larson, in his book *Wind and Fire*, points out some interesting facts about sandhill cranes:

"These large birds, who fly great distances across continents, have three remarkable qualities. First, they rotate leadership. No one bird stays out in front all the time. Second, they choose leaders who can handle turbulence. And then, all during the time one bird is leading, the rest are honking their affirmation."

"Without wise leadership a nation falls; with many counsellors, there is safety."
The Bible, Proverbs 11:14

The captain of a floundering ship does little good by criticising the crew to the passengers.

Caution to newly promoted executives – remember what the mamma whale told the baby whale: "When you get to the top and start letting off steam, that's the time you're most apt to be harpooned."

Leisure

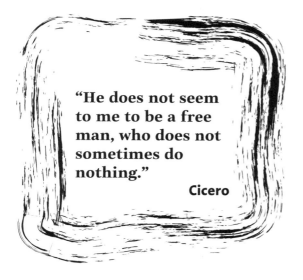

"He does not seem to me to be a free man, who does not sometimes do nothing."

Cicero

Instructed to make sure his squad got some time off, the drill sergeant lined them up and barked, "Relax! That's an order!"

"Leisure is the mother of philosophy."

Thomas Hobbes

People's worth should be judged by what they do when they don't have to be doing anything.

Life

"The purpose of life is to find out who am I? Why am I here? Where am I going? That's what we need answering."

George Harrison

The secret of life is not to do what you like but to like what you do.

"The more science learns what life is, the more reluctant scientists are to define it."

Leila Coyne

"The first forty years of life give us the text; the next thirty supply the commentary."

Arthur Schopenhauer

"Let us endeavour to live so that when we come to die, even the undertaker will be sorry."

Mark Twain

One day a farmer's donkey fell down a well. The animal cried piteously for hours as the farmer tried to figure out what to do. Finally he decided the animal was old and the well needed to be covered up anyway, it just wasn't worth it to retrieve the donkey. So he invited all his neighbours to come over and help him. They all grabbed a shovel and began to shovel dirt into the well. At first, the donkey realised what was happening and cried horribly. Then, to everyone's amazement, he quietened down. A few shovel loads later, the farmer finally looked down the well and was astonished at what he saw. With every shovel of dirt that hit his back, the donkey was doing something amazing. He would shake it off and take a step up. As the farmer's neighbours continued to shovel dirt on top of the animal, he would shake it off and take a step up. Pretty soon, everyone was amazed as the donkey stepped up over the edge of the well and trotted off!

Moral: Life is going to shovel dirt on you, all kinds of dirt. The trick to getting out of the well is to shake it off and take a step up. Each of our troubles is a stepping stone. We can get out of the deepest wells just by not stopping, never giving up! Shake it off and take a step up!

I read of a man who stood to speak
at the funeral of his friend.
He referred to the dates on her tombstone
from the beginning…to the end.
He noted that first came the date of her birth
and spoke of the second with tears,
but he said that what mattered most of all
was the dash between those years.
For that dash represents all the time
that she spent alive on earth,
and now only those who loved her
know what that little line is worth.
For it matters not, how much we own;
the cars, the house, the cash.
What matters is how we live and love
and how we spend our dash.
So think about this long and hard,
are there things you'd like to change?
For you never know how much time is left.
(You could be at "dash mid-range".)
If we could just slow down enough to consider
what's true and what's real,
and always try to understand
the way other people feel.
And…be less quick to anger,
and show appreciation more
and love the people in our lives
like we've never loved before.
If we treat each other with respect,
and more often wear a smile,
remembering that this special dash
might only last a little while.
So, when your eulogy is being read
with your life's actions to rehash…
would you be pleased with the things they say
about how you spent your dash?

Anon

Someone has calculated how a typical lifespan of 70 years is spent. Here is the estimate:

Sleep	23 years	32.9%
Work	16 years	22.8%
TV	8 years	11.4%
Eating	6 years	8.6%
Travel	6 years	8.6%
Leisure	4.5 years	6.5%
Illness	4 years	5.7%
Dressing	2 years	2.8%
Religion	0.5 years	0.7%
Total	70 years	100%

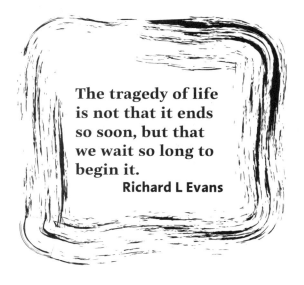

The tragedy of life is not that it ends so soon, but that we wait so long to begin it.
Richard L Evans

The seven ages of man: spills, drills, thrills, bills, ills, pills, wills.
Richard J Needham

Light

Making decisions in the dark can lead to some regrettable consequences. Back in the days before electricity, a tightfisted old farmer was taking his hired man to task for carrying a lighted lantern when he went to call on his best girl. "Why," he exclaimed, "when I went a-courtin' I never carried one of them things. I always went in the dark."

"Yes," the hired man said wryly, "and look what you got!"

*Some people change their ways
when they see the light, others
only when they feel the heat.*

Listening

"When you talk, you repeat what you already know. When you listen, you often learn something."

Jaren Sparks

All speech, written or spoken, is a dead language, until it finds a willing and prepared listener.

Robert Louis Stevenson

The grace of listening is lost if the listener's attention is demanded, not as a favour, but as a right.

Pliny the Younger

"One friend, one person who is truly understanding, who takes the trouble to listen to us as we consider a problem, can change our whole outlook on the world."

Dr E H Mayo

A pair of good ears will drain dry a hundred tongues.

The greatest gift you can give another is the purity of your attention.

Richard Moss

Easy listening exists only on the radio.

David Barkan

God still speaks to those who take time to listen.

"Give us grace to listen well."
John Keble

Looking for the solution without listening to the problem is working in the dark.

The truth which makes us free is for the most part the truth which we prefer not to hear.
James Bishop

"As friends, we don't see eye to eye, but then we don't hear ear to ear either."
Buster Keaton

It is the province of knowledge to speak and it is the privilege of wisdom to listen.
Oliver Wendell Holmes

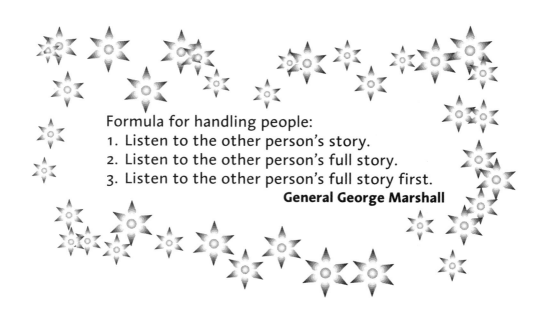

Formula for handling people:
1. Listen to the other person's story.
2. Listen to the other person's full story.
3. Listen to the other person's full story first.
General George Marshall

> **G**ood listening is like tuning in a radio station. For good results, you can listen to only one station at a time. Trying to listen to my wife while looking over an office report is like trying to receive two radio stations at the same time. I end up with distortion and frustration. Listening requires a choice of where I place my attention. To tune into my partner, I must first choose to put away all that will divide my attention. That might mean laying down the newspaper, moving away from the dishes in the sink, putting down the book I'm reading, setting aside my projects.
>
> **Robert W Herron**

Love

It is easier to love humanity as a whole than to love one's neighbour.
Eric Hoffer

"Love is the basic need of human nature, for without it life is disrupted emotionally, mentally, spiritually and physically."
Dr Karl Menninger

Love is a fabric that never fades, no matter how often it is washed in the waters of adversity and grief.

"Tis better to have loved and lost Than never to have loved at all."
Tennyson

"The supreme happiness of life is the conviction that we are loved."
Victor Hugo

"The first duty of love is to listen."
Paul Tillich

In the musical *Fiddler on the Roof*, Tevye, a man devoted to tradition, finds his thinking challenged when his oldest daughter wants to marry for love, instead of having her marriage arranged by her parents.

It had never occurred to him that one would marry for love, and one night he cannot help but ask his own wife the question (in song, of course!): "Do You Love Me?"

T: Golde, do you love me?
G: Do I what?
T: Do you love me?
G: You're a fool!
T: I know! But do you love me?

G: Do I love him? For twenty-five years I've cooked for him, cleaned for him, starved with him. Twenty-five years my bed is his. If that's not love – what is?

Newspaper columnist and minister George Crane tells of a wife who came into his office full of hatred toward her husband. "I do not only want to get rid of him, I want to get even. Before I divorce him, I want to hurt him as much as he has me."

Dr Crane suggested an ingenious plan: "Go home and act as if you really love your husband. Tell him how much he means to you. Praise him for every decent trait. Go out of your way to be as kind, considerate, and generous as possible. Spare no efforts to please him, to enjoy him. Make him believe you love him. After you've convinced him of your undying love and that you cannot live without him, then drop the bomb. Tell him that you're getting a divorce. That will really hurt him."

With revenge in her eyes, she smiled and exclaimed, "Beautiful, beautiful. Will he ever be surprised!"

And she did it with enthusiasm. Acting "as if". For two months she showed love, kindness, listening, giving, reinforcing, sharing.

When she didn't return, Crane called. "Are you ready now to go through with the divorce?"

"Divorce?" she exclaimed. "Never! I discovered I really do love him." Her actions had changed her feelings.

Ted Stallard undoubtedly qualified as one of "the least". Turned off by school. Very sloppy in appearance. Expressionless. Unattractive. Even his teacher, Miss Thompson, enjoyed wielding her red pen as she placed Xs beside his many wrong answers.

If only she had studied his records more carefully. They read:

1st grade: Ted shows promise with his work and attitude, but (has) poor home situation.

2nd grade: Ted could do better. Mother seriously ill. Receives little help from home.

3rd grade: Ted is good boy but too serious. He is a slow learner. His mother died this year.

4th grade: Ted is very slow, but well-behaved. His father shows no interest whatsoever.

Christmas arrived. The children piled elaborately wrapped gifts on their teacher's desk. Ted brought one too. It was wrapped in brown paper and held together with Scotch Tape. Miss Thompson opened each gift, as the children crowded around to watch. Out of Ted's package fell a gaudy rhinestone bracelet, with half of the stones missing, and a bottle of cheap perfume. The children began to snicker. But she silenced them by splashing some of the perfume on her wrist, and letting them smell it. She put the bracelet on too.

At day's end, after the other children had left, Ted came by the teacher's desk and said, "Miss Thompson, you smell just like my mother. And the bracelet looks real pretty on you. I'm glad you like my presents." He left. Miss Thompson got down on her knees and asked God to forgive her and to change her attitude.

The next term, the children were greeted by a reformed teacher — one committed to loving each of them. Especially the slow ones. Especially Ted. Surprisingly – or maybe, not surprisingly – Ted began to show great improvement. He actually caught up with most of the students and even passed a few.

Time came and went. Miss Thompson heard nothing from Ted for a long time. Then, one day, she received this note:

> Dear Miss Thompson,
>   I wanted you to be the first to know. I will be graduating second in my class.
>   Love, Ted

Four years later, another note arrived:

> Dear Miss Thompson,
>   They just told me I will be graduating first in my class. I wanted you to be the first to know. The university has not been easy, but I liked it.
>   Love, Ted

And four years later:

> Dear Miss Thompson,
>   As of today, I am Theodore Stallard, MD. How about that? I wanted you to be the first to know. I am getting married next month, the 27th to be exact. I want you to come and sit where my mother would sit if she were alive. You are the only family I have now; Dad died last year.

Miss Thompson attended that wedding, and sat where Ted's mother would have sat. The compassion she had shown that young man entitled her to that privilege.

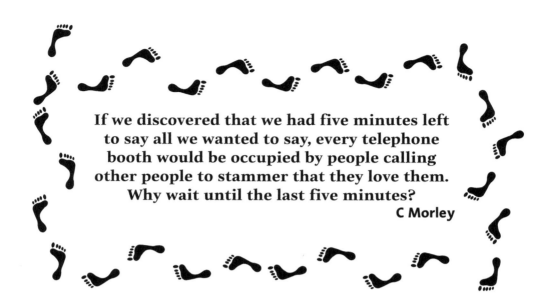

If we discovered that we had five minutes left to say all we wanted to say, every telephone booth would be occupied by people calling other people to stammer that they love them. Why wait until the last five minutes?

C Morley

Love-letter lament:

Dearest Jimmy,
    No words could ever express the great unhappiness I've felt since breaking our engagement. Please say you'll take me back. No one could ever take your place in my heart, so please forgive me. I love you, I love you, I love you!

Yours forever,
Marie

P.S. And congratulations on winning the lottery.

A young man said to his father at breakfast one morning, "Dad, I'm going to get married."

"How do you know you're ready to get married?" asked the father. "Are you in love?"

"I sure am," said the son.

"How do you know you're in love?" asked the father.

"Last night as I was kissing my girlfriend goodnight, her dog bit me and I didn't feel the pain until I got home."

Management

A man in a hot air balloon realised he was lost. He reduced altitude and spotted a woman below. He descended a bit more and shouted, "Excuse me, can you help me? I promised a friend I would meet him an hour ago, but I don't know where I am."

The woman below replied, "You are in a hot air balloon hovering approximately 30 feet above the ground. You are between 40 and 41 degrees north latitude and between 59 and 60 degrees west longitude."

"You must be an engineer," said the balloonist.

"I am," replied the woman. "How did you know?"

"Well," answered the balloonist, "everything you told me is technically correct, but I have no idea what to make of your information, and the fact is I am still lost. Frankly, you've not been much help so far."

The woman below responded, "You must be in management."

"I am," replied the balloonist, "but how did you know?"

"Well," said the woman, "you don't know where you are or where you are going. You have risen to where you are, due to a large quantity of hot air. You made a promise which you have no idea how to keep, and you expect people beneath you to solve your problems. The fact is you are in exactly the same position you were in before we met, but now, somehow, it's my fault."

"Good management consists in showing average people how to do the work of superior people."

John D Rockefeller

"I don't want any yes people around me. I want everybody to tell me the truth, even if it costs them their jobs."

Samuel Goldwyn

"Never try to teach a pig to sing; it wastes your time and it annoys the pig."

John Paul Getty

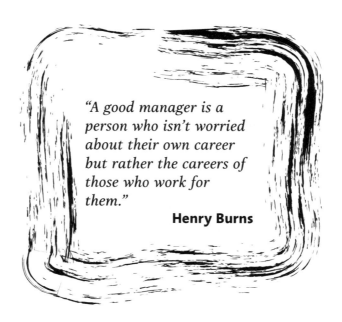

"A good manager is a person who isn't worried about their own career but rather the careers of those who work for them."

Henry Burns

A person who works with their hands is a labourer.
A person who works with their hands and brains is a craftsman.
A person who works with their brains and the hands of others is
    an executive.

A short course in human relations:

The six most important words: I admit that I was wrong.
The five most important words: you did a great job.
The four most important words: what do you think?
The three most important words: could you please…?
The two most important words: thank you.
The most important word: we
The least important word: I

> *"If you command wisely, you'll be obeyed cheerfully."*
> **Thomas Fuller**

Marriage

How does a typical husband respond when his wife comes down with a cold?

In the first year of marriage: "Darling, I'm really worried about my baby girl. You've got a bad sniffle, and there's no telling about these things with all the terrible viruses going around these days. I've called the emergency doctor, and I've called your mum and she's coming to help with the cooking and cleaning."

Second year of marriage: "Listen, darling, I don't like the sound of that cough and I've made an appointment with the doctor. Now you go to bed like a good girl, and I'll take care of everything."

Third year: "Maybe you'd better lie down, darling. Nothing like a little rest when you're feeling lousy. I'll bring you something. Do we have any canned soup?"

Fourth year: "Now look dear, be sensible. After you feed the kids, do the dishes and mop the floor, you better get some rest."

Fifth year: "Why don't you take a couple of aspirin?"

Sixth year: "If you'd just gargle or something, instead of sitting around barking like a seal all night…"

Seventh year: "For Pete's sake, stop sneezing! What are you trying to do, give me pneumonia?"

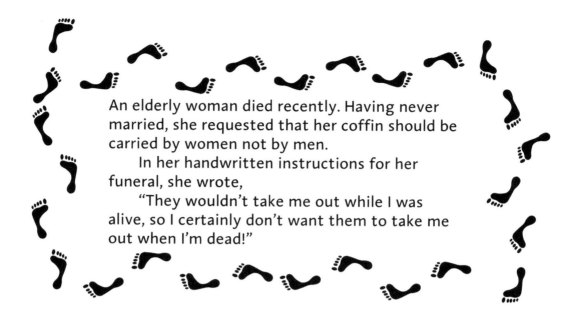

An elderly woman died recently. Having never married, she requested that her coffin should be carried by women not by men.

In her handwritten instructions for her funeral, she wrote,

"They wouldn't take me out while I was alive, so I certainly don't want them to take me out when I'm dead!"

A woman accompanied her husband to the doctor's office. After his check up, the doctor called the wife into his office alone.

He said, "Your husband is suffering from a very serious disease, combined with horrible stress. If you don't do the following, your husband can die. Each morning, fix him a healthy breakfast. Be pleasant and make sure he is in a good mood. For lunch, fix him a nutritious meal. For dinner, prepare an especially nice meal for him. Don't burden him with chores. Don't discuss your stress; this will probably make him feel worse.

If you can do this for at least ten months to a year, I think your husband will regain his health completely."

On the way home, the husband asked his wife, "What did the doctor say to you?"

"You're going to die."

A couple drove several miles down a country road, not saying a word. An earlier discussion had led to an argument, and neither wanted to concede their position. As they passed a barnyard of mules and pigs, the husband sarcastically asked,

"Relatives of yours?"

"Yep," the wife replied, "in-laws."

Have you ever wondered if the Bible has any tips on how to find the girl of your dreams? Good news! There are numerous biblical examples for you to consider:

1. Find an attractive prisoner of war, bring her home, shave her head, trim her nails, and give her new clothes. Then she's yours. (Deuteronomy 21:11–13)
2. Find a prostitute and marry her. (Hosea 1:1–3)
3. Find a man with seven daughters and impress him by watering his flock. (Moses – Exodus 2:16–21)
4. Purchase a piece of property and get a woman as part of the deal. (Boaz – Ruth 4:5–10)
5. Go to a party and hide. When the women come out to dance, grab one and carry her off to be your wife. (Judges 21:19–25)
6. Have God create a wife for you while you sleep. But be careful; it'll cost you a rib (Adam – Genesis 2:19–24)
7. Agree to work seven years in exchange for a woman's hand in marriage. Get tricked into marrying the wrong woman, then work another seven years for the woman you wanted to marry in the first place. That's right. Fourteen years of hard labour for a wife. (Jacob – Genesis 29:15–30)
8. Cut 200 foreskins off the enemies of your future father-in-law and get his daughter in exchange. (David – 1 Samuel 18:27)
9. Even if no one is out there, just wander around a bit and you'll find someone. Maybe your sister. (Cain – Genesis 4:16–17)
10. Become the emperor of a huge nation and hold a beauty contest. (Xerxes – Esther 2:3–4)
11. When you see someone you like, go home and tell your parents, "I have seen a woman I like. Now get her for me." If your parents question your decision, simply say, "Get her for me. She's the one for me." (Samson – Judges 14:1–3)
12. Kill any husband and take his wife. (David – 2 Samuel 11)
13. Wait for your brother to die, then take his widow. It's not just a good idea; it's the law. (Deuteronomy and Leviticus, example of Boaz in Ruth)

The speaker at a women's club was lecturing on marriage and asked the audience how many of them wanted to "mother" their husbands. One member in the back row raised her hand.

"You do want to mother your husband?" the speaker asked.

"Mother?" the woman echoed. "I thought you said smother."

More and more people seem to forget Henry Ford's sage advice when asked on his 50th wedding anniversary for his rule for marital bliss and longevity. He replied, "Just the same as in the automobile business, stick to one model."

On her golden wedding anniversary, my grandmother revealed the secret of her long and happy marriage. "On my wedding day, I decided to choose ten of my husband's faults which, for the sake of our marriage, I would overlook," she explained. A guest asked her to name some of the faults. "To tell the truth," she replied, "I never did get around to listing them. But whenever my husband did something that made me hopping mad, I would say to myself, 'Lucky for him that's one of the ten.'"

A Prayer for a Married Couple

O God, our Heavenly Father, protect and bless us. Deepen and strengthen our love for each other day by day. Grant that by Thy mercy neither of us ever say one unkind word to the other. Forgive and correct our faults, and make us constantly to forgive one another should one of us unconsciously hurt the other. Make us and keep us sound and well in body, alert in mind, tender in heart, devout in spirit. O Lord, grant us each to rise to the other's best. Then we pray Thee add to our common life such virtues as only Thou canst give. And so, O Father, consecrate our life and our love completely to Thy worship, and to the service of all about us, especially those whom Thou has appointed us to serve, that we may always stand before Thee in happiness and peace; through Jesus Christ our Lord. Amen.

Bishop Slattery

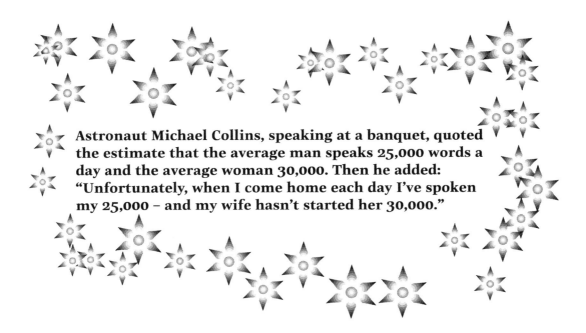

Astronaut Michael Collins, speaking at a banquet, quoted the estimate that the average man speaks 25,000 words a day and the average woman 30,000. Then he added: "Unfortunately, when I come home each day I've spoken my 25,000 – and my wife hasn't started her 30,000."

Wife, just coming home, to husband:
"I've been to karate class, so dinner will
be late. Want to make something of it?"

A good marriage is the union of two forgivers.
Ruth Bell Graham

One woman to another at the office, "Did you wake up grouchy today?"

"No, I just let him sleep in."

Love, the quest;
Marriage, the conquest;
Divorce, the inquest.
Helen Rowland

Before you marry, keep your two eyes open; after you marry, shut one.
Jamaican proverb

Twelve Rules for a Happy Marriage:

1.   Never both be angry at once.

2.   Never yell at each other unless the house is on fire.

3.   Remember that it takes two to make an argument. The one who is wrong is the one who will be doing most of the talking.

4.   Yield to the wishes of the other – as an exercise in self-discipline, if you can't think of a better reason.

5.   If you have a choice between making yourself or your mate look good – choose your mate.

6.   If you feel you must criticise, do so lovingly.

7.   Never bring up a mistake of the past.

8.   Neglect the whole world rather than each other.

9.   Never let the day end without saying at least one complimentary thing to your life partner.

10. Never meet without an affectionate greeting.

11. When you've made a mistake, talk it out and ask for forgiveness.

12. Never go to bed angry.

Ann Landers

Men and Women

One day, three men were hiking and unexpectedly came upon a large raging, violent river. They needed to get to the other side, but had no idea of how to do so.

The first man prayed to God, saying, "Please God, give me the strength to cross this river." Poof! God gave him big arms and strong legs, and he was able to swim across the river in about two hours, after almost drowning a couple of times.

Seeing this, the second man prayed to God, saying, "Please God, give me the strength and the tools to cross this river." Poof! God gave him a rowboat and he was able to row across the river in about an hour, after almost capsizing the boat a couple of times.

The third man had seen how this worked out for the other two, so he also prayed to God saying, "Please God, give me the strength and the tools…and the intelligence…to cross this river." And poof! God turned him into a woman.

She looked at the map, hiked upstream a couple of hundred yards, then walked across the bridge.

Are you tired of the battle between the sexes? Men and women are different. There's no question about it. But instead of focusing on the negative qualities of men and women, why not celebrate their positive qualities? Let's start with the Women:

- Women are compassionate, and loving, and caring.
- Women cry when they are happy.
- Women are always doing little things to show they care.
- They will stop at nothing to get what they think is best for their children (best school, best dress, best dentist).
- Women have the ability to keep smiling when they are so tired they can hardly stand up.
- They know how to turn a simple meal into an occasion.
- Women know how to get the most for their money.
- They know how to comfort a sick friend.
- Women bring joy and laughter to the world.
- They know how to entertain children for hours on end!
- They are honest and loyal.
- Women have a will of iron under that soft exterior.
- They will go the extra mile to help a friend in need.
- Women are easily brought to tears by injustice.
- They know how to make a man feel like a king.
- Women make the world a much happier place to live in.

Now, for the Men:

- Men are good at moving heavy things and removing spiders.

On a transatlantic flight, a plane passes through a severe storm. The turbulence is awful, and things go from bad to worse when one wing is struck by lightning.

One woman loses it. Screaming, she wails, "I'm too young to die."

Then she yells, "Well, if I'm going to die, I want my last minutes on earth to be memorable! Is there ANYONE on this plane who can make me feel like a WOMAN?"

For a moment there is silence. Everyone has forgotten their own peril. They all stare, riveted, at the desperate woman in the front of the plane. Then a man stands up in the rear of the plane. He is gorgeous, tall, well-built, with reddish-blond hair and hazel eyes. He starts to walk slowly up the aisle, unbuttoning his shirt... one button at a time.

No one moves.

He removes his shirt.

Muscles ripple across his chest.

He whispers:

"Iron this."

While on a long car journey, a couple stopped at a roadside restaurant for lunch. The woman unfortunately left her sunglasses on the table, but didn't miss them until they were back on the motorway. By then, they had to travel to the next junction before they could turn around.

The man fussed and complained all the way back to the restaurant.

When they finally arrived, as the woman got out of the car to find her sunglasses, the man said, "While you're in there, you may as well get my hat, too."

Mistakes

God has a big eraser.

"It is very easy to forgive others their mistakes. It takes more guts and gumption to forgive them for having witnessed your own."
Jessamyn West

"The greatest mistake you can make in life is to be continually fearing you will make one."
Elbert Hubbard

Anyone can make a mistake; only a fool will persist in it.

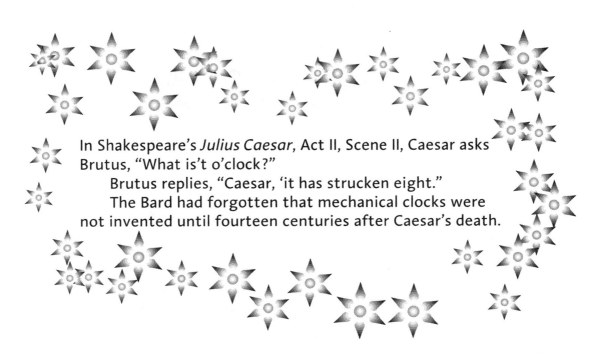

In Shakespeare's *Julius Caesar*, Act II, Scene II, Caesar asks Brutus, "What is't o'clock?"

Brutus replies, "Caesar, 'it has strucken eight."

The Bard had forgotten that mechanical clocks were not invented until fourteen centuries after Caesar's death.

It doesn't matter how much milk you spill so long as you don't lose the cow.

Morality

In his 1983 acceptance speech for the Templeton Prize for Progress in Religion, Solzhenitsyn recalled the words he heard as a child, when his elders sought to explain the ruinous upheavals in Russia: "Men have forgotten God; that's why all this has happened." He added, "If I were called upon to identify briefly the principal trait of the entire twentieth century, here too I would be unable to find anything more precise and pithy than to repeat once again: 'Men have forgotten God.'"

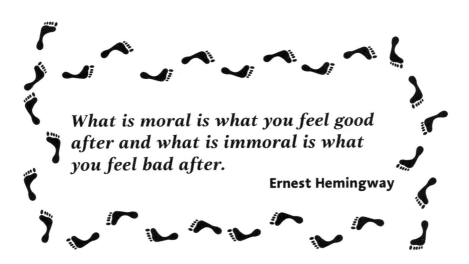

What is moral is what you feel good after and what is immoral is what you feel bad after.

Ernest Hemingway

Motherhood

A teacher asked a boy this question:

"Suppose your mother baked a pie and there were seven of you – your parents and five children. What part of the pie would you get?"

"A sixth," replied the boy.

"I'm afraid you don't know your fractions," said the teacher. "Remember, there are seven of you."

"Yes, teacher," said the boy, "but you don't know my mother. Mother would say she didn't want any pie."

Dear Child,

The Bathroom Door is Closed!

Please do not stand here and talk, whine, or ask questions.

Wait until I get out.

Yes, it is locked. I want it that way. It is not broken, and I am not trapped.

I know I have left it unlocked, and even open at times, since you were born, because I was afraid some horrible tragedy might occur while I was in there, but it's been ten years and I want some PRIVACY.

Do not ask me how long I will be. I will come out when I am done.

Do not bring the phone to the bathroom door.

Do not go running back to the phone yelling "She's on the toilet!"

Do not stick your little fingers under the door and wiggle them. This was funny when you were two.

Do not slide pennies, LEGOs, or notes under the door.

If you have followed me down the hall talking, and are still talking as you face this closed door, please turn around, walk away, and wait for me in another room. I will be glad to listen to you when I am done.

And yes, I still love you,

MUM

The most creative job in the world involves fashion, decorating, recreation, education, transportation, psychology, romance, cuisine, literature, art, economics, government, pediatrics, geriatrics, entertainment, maintenance, purchasing, law, religion, energy and management. Anyone who can handle all those has to be somebody special. She's a homemaker.

Richard Kerr

A four-year-old and a six-year-old presented their mum with a house plant. They had used their own money and she was thrilled. The elder of them said with a sad face, "There was a bouquet that we wanted to give you at the flower shop. It was real pretty, but it was too expensive. It had a ribbon on it that said, 'Rest In Peace', and we thought it would be just perfect since you are always asking for a little peace so that you can rest."

The mother of three notoriously unruly teenagers was asked whether or not she'd have children if she had it to do over again. "Yes," she replied. "But not the same ones."

Music

J S Bach said, "All music should have no other end and aim than the glory of God and the soul's refreshment; where this is not remembered there is no real music but only a devilish hub-bub."

He headed his compositions: "J J" "Jesus Juva" which means "Jesus help me".

He ended them "S D G" "Soli Dei gratia" which means "To God alone the praise".

Mystery

Oliver Wendell Holmes, Senior, was a doctor. As such he was very interested in the use of ether. In order to know how his patients felt under its influence, he once had a dose administered to himself.

As he was going under, in a dreamy state, a profound thought came to him. He believed that he had suddenly grasped the key to all the mysteries of the universe. When he regained consciousness, however, he was unable to remember what the insight was.

Because of the great importance this thought would be to humankind, Holmes arranged to have himself given ether again. This time he had a stenographer present to take down the great thought. The ether was administered, and sure enough, just before passing out the insight reappeared. He mumbled the words, the stenographer took them down, and he went to sleep confident in the knowledge that he had succeeded.

Upon awakening, he turned eagerly to the stenographer and asked her to read what he had uttered. This is what she read: "The entire universe is permeated with a strong odour of turpentine."

N

Names

A woman – heavily pregnant with twins – was involved in a car crash and went into a coma. While she was unconscious her twins were delivered.

When she came round the nurse told her that she had twins and that her brother was now looking after them until she was well enough to go home.

"Not my brother!" the woman exclaimed. "He's a complete imbecile."

"It's all right," said the nurse. "He seems to be doing a really good job. He's even given them names."

"You're kidding!" said the mother. "What's he called them?"

"Well, I think he's called the girl Denise."

"Oh, that doesn't sound so bad after all," said the mother. "What's he called the boy?"

"De Nephew," replied the nurse.

Noise

"Carry some quiet around inside thee," the well-known Quaker, George Fox, used to say. "Be still and cool in thy own mind and spirit, from thy own thoughts, and then thou wilt feel the principle of God to turn thy mind to the Lord from whence cometh life; whereby thou mayest receive the strength and power to allay all storms and tempests."

Oratory is the fine art of making deep noises from the chest sound like important messages from the brain.

"Most people lead lives of noisy desperation."
James Thurber

"Beethoven's Fifth Symphony is the most sublime noise that has ever penetrated into the ear of man."
E M Forster

Noise proves nothing. Often a hen who has merely laid an egg cackles as if she had laid an asteroid.

Mark Twain

Obedience

In the eleventh century, King Henry III of Bavaria grew tired of court life and the pressures of being a monarch. He made an application to Prior Richard at a local monastery, asking to be accepted as a contemplative and spend the rest of his life in the monastery. "Your Majesty," said Prior Richard, "do you understand that the pledge here is one of obedience? That will be hard because you have been a king."

"I understand," said Henry. "The rest of my life I will be obedient to you, as Christ leads you."

"Then I will tell you what to do," said Prior Richard. "Go back to your throne and serve faithfully in the place where God has put you."

When King Henry died, a statement was written: "The King learned to rule by being obedient." When we tire of our roles and responsibilities, it helps to remember God has planted us in a certain place and told us to be a good accountant or teacher or mother or father.

Obstacles

"When everything seems to be going against you, remember the aircraft takes off against the wind, not with it."
Henry Ford

"Real difficulties can be overcome; it is only the imaginary ones that are unconquerable."
Theodore N Vail

Don't fix the blame, fix the problem.

If you want a place in the sun, you've got to expect a few blisters.

"Problems are only opportunities in work clothes."
Henry Kaiser

"It is only because of problems that we grow mentally and spiritually."
M Scott Peck

Noah, despite a strange assignment and the likely ridicule of his neighbours, obeyed God and built the boat that would preserve life on Earth. (Genesis 6 – 9)

Joseph, despite numerous personal tragedies, became the preserver and protector of the fledgling nation of Israel. (Genesis 37 – 50)

Moses, despite a deep sense of inadequacy, became the liberator, lawgiver, and leader of the Israelites. (Exodus 2 – Deuteronomy 34)

Caleb, despite being "over the hill" at 85, asked for and received the opportunity to defeat the Anakite peoples living near Hebron. (Joshua 14 – 15)

Deborah, despite being a woman (a position lacking respect in her day), led God's people to victory over their enemies. (Judges 4:4–14)

Gideon, despite great fear and overwhelming odds, led the Israelites in defeating their Midianite oppressors. (Judges 6 – 8)

David, despite his youth, the scorn of his brothers, and formidable opponent, defeated the dreaded Goliath and showed his mettle as a man after God's heart. (1 Samuel 16 – 17)

Nathan, despite the possibility of retribution from King David, confronted David with his sins of adultery and murder. (2 Samuel 12)

Josiah, despite having an evil father and grandfather, became a great reformer, turning the nation of Judah back to God. (2 Kings 22 – 23)

Esther, despite being young and a foreigner, became queen and saved God's people. (Esther 2 – 9)

Jeremiah, despite criticism, unpopularity and attacks against him, faithfully delivered God's message to the nation of Judah. (Jeremiah and Lamentations)

Daniel, despite exile, opposition, and an encounter with some ravenous lions, faithfully served and represented God before the most powerful world leaders of his time. (Daniel 1 – 12)

John the Baptist, despite being misunderstood and having occasional doubts, pointed others to Christ. (Matthew 3:11)

Mary, despite being a teenager, became the mother of Jesus Christ who is the son of God and Saviour of the World. (Luke 1 – 2)

Mary Magdalene, despite once being possessed by seven demons, became a faithful follower of Jesus and told the disciples that Jesus had been raised from the dead. (Mark 16:9–11, Luke 24:1–2)

Peter, despite a history of painful public failures, became the most visible and vocal leader of the early church. (John 18 – 21, Acts 1 – 12)

Paul, despite having been a bitter enemy of Christianity, became the foremost spokesman and apologist for the gospel. (Acts 9 – 28)

Optimism

During his days as president, Thomas Jefferson and a group of companions were travelling across the country on horseback. They came to a river which had broken its banks because of a recent downpour. The swollen river had washed the bridge away. Each rider was forced to ford the river on horseback, fighting for his life against the rapid currents. The very real possibility of death threatened each rider, which caused a traveller who was not part of their group to step aside and watch. After several had plunged in and made it to the other side, the stranger asked President Jefferson if he would ferry him across the river. The president agreed without hesitation. The man climbed on, and shortly thereafter the two of them made it safely to the other side.

As the stranger slid off the back of the saddle onto dry ground, one in the group asked him, "Tell me, why did you select the president to ask this favour of?"

The man was shocked, admitting he had no idea it was the president who had helped him. "All I know," he said, "is that on some of your faces was written the answer 'No', and on some of them was the answer 'Yes'. His was a 'Yes' face."

A child psychologist wanted to observe how different children respond to negative circumstances.

They filled a room with horse manure. Putting a pessimistic child in there, they observed how he responded.

Predictably, he whined and cried, and despaired that he was in a room full of smelly manure.

They put an optimistic child in there, and he started tearing around the room, digging in the manure with an excitement that baffled the on-lookers.

After a few moments of watching this, they asked him why he was so excited.

He replied, "With all this manure in the room, there's got to be a pony in here somewhere!"

P

Peace

How to get inner peace...

The way to achieve inner peace is to finish things you've started. It is definitely working for me. I am now making a point of always finishing what I start and I think I am well on my way toward finding inner peace.

Because I care for you, I am passing this wisdom on to you. Here are the things that I have finished today:

> two bags of crisps
> a strawberry cheesecake
> a packet of biscuits
> a bottle of coke
> a small box of chocolates

Perseverance

If I have ever made any valuable discoveries, it has been owing more to patient attention, than to any other talent.

Isaac Newton

Never give in! Never give in! Never! Never! Never! Never! In anything great or small, large or petty – never give in except to convictions of honour and good sense.

Winston Churchill

Perseverance is the most overrated of traits: if it is unaccompanied by talent, beating your head against a wall is more likely to produce a concussion in the head than a hole in the wall.
Sydney J Harris

Prayer

May you get a clean bill of health from your dentist, your cardiologist, your gastro-endocrinologist, your urologist, your proctologist, your podiatrist, your psychiatrist, your gynaecologist, your plumber and the taxman.

May your hair, your teeth, your face-lift, your abs and your stocks not fall; and may your blood pressure, your triglycerides, your cholesterol, your white blood count and your mortgage interest not rise.

Prayer is an offering up of our desires unto God, for things agreeable to His will, in the name of Christ, with confession of our sins, and thankful acknowledgement of His mercies.
Westminster Shorter Catechism

He who runs from God in the morning will scarcely find Him the rest of the day.
John Bunyan

Life is fragile; handle with prayer.

Pray as if everything depends on God, then work as if everything depends on you.

Martin Luther

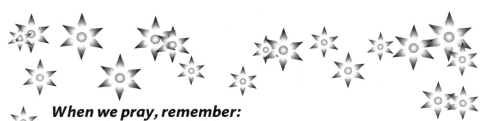

When we pray, remember:
1. *The love of God that wants the best for us.*
2. *The wisdom of God that knows what is best for us.*
3. *The power of God that can accomplish it.*

William Barclay

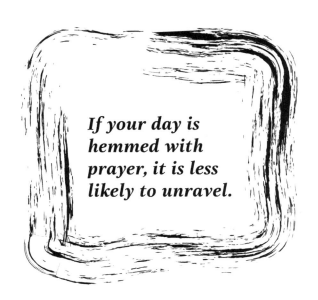

If your day is hemmed with prayer, it is less likely to unravel.

A friend took his small son with him to town one day to run some errands. When lunchtime arrived, the two of them went to a familiar cafe for a sandwich. The father sat down on one of the stools at the counter and lifted the boy up to the seat beside him. They ordered lunch, and when the waiter brought the food, the father said, "Son, we'll just have a silent prayer." Dad got through praying first and waited for the boy to finish his prayer, but he just sat with his head bowed for an unusually long time. When he finally looked up, his father asked him, "What in the world were you praying about all that time?" With the innocence and honesty of a child, he replied, "How do I know? It was a silent prayer."

If the request is wrong, God says, "No."
If the timing is wrong, God says, "Slow."
If you are wrong, God says, "Grow."
But if the request is right, the timing is right and you are right, God says, "Go!"

Bill Hybels

Five young college students were spending a Sunday in London, so they went to hear the famed C H Spurgeon preach. While waiting for the doors to open, the students were greeted by a man who asked, "Gentlemen, let me show you around. Would you like to see the heating plant of this church?" They were not particularly interested, for it was a hot day in July. But they didn't want to offend the stranger, so they consented. The young men were taken down a stairway, a door was quietly opened, and their guide whispered, "This is our heating plant." Surprised, the students saw 700 people bowed in prayer, seeking a blessing on the service that was soon to begin in the auditorium above. Softly closing the door, the gentleman then introduced himself. It was none other than Charles Spurgeon.

Things looked bleak for the children of George Müller's orphanage at Ashley Downs in England. It was time for breakfast, and there was no food. A small girl whose father was a close friend of Müller was visiting the home. Müller took her hand and said, "Come and see what our Father will do." In the dining room, long tables were set with empty plates and empty mugs. Not only was there no food in the kitchen, but there was no money in the home's account. Müller prayed, "Dear Father, we thank Thee for what Thou art going to give us to eat." Immediately, they heard a knock at the door. When they opened it, there stood the local baker. "Mr Müller," he said, "I couldn't sleep last night. Somehow I felt you had no bread for breakfast, so I got up at two o'clock and baked fresh bread. Here it is." Müller thanked him and gave praise to God. Soon, a second knock was heard. It was the milkman. His cart had broken down in front of the orphanage. He said he would like to give the children the milk so he could empty the cart and repair it.

When everything seems to go wrong…just P.U.S.H!
When the job gets you down…just P.U.S.H!
When people don't react the way you think they should…just P.U.S.H!
When your money is gone and the bills are due…just P.U.S.H!
When people just don't understand you…just P.U.S.H!

P = Pray
U = Until
S = Something
H = Happens

Prayers

> Lord,
> Be Thou within me, to strengthen me;
> Without me, to keep me;
> Above me, to protect me;
> Beneath me, to uphold me;
> Before me, to direct me;
> Behind me, to keep me from straying;
> Round about me, to defend me.
> Blessed be Thou, O Lord, our Father,
> for ever and ever.
> **Lancelot Andrewes (1555–1626)**

Preaching

"I hope you didn't take it personally, Reverend," an embarrassed woman said after a church service, "when my husband walked out during your sermon."

"I did find it rather disconcerting," the minister replied.

"It's not a reflection on you, sir," insisted the churchgoer. "Ralph has been walking in his sleep ever since he was a child."

President Calvin Coolidge, 30th US president (1923–1929) was a man of very few words. One Sunday he went to church, but his wife, Grace, stayed home. When he returned, she asked, "Was the sermon good?"

"Yup," was Coolidge's brief reply.

"What was it about?" Grace asked.

"Sin."

"And what did the minister say?"

"He's against it."

There was a preacher who entered his pulpit one Sunday morning and said:

"Oh, Lord, give thy servant this mornin' the eyes of the eagle and the wisdom of the owl; connect his soul with the gospel telephone in the central skies; illuminate his brow with the Sun of Heaven; possess his mind with love for the people; turpentine his imagination; grease his lips with possum oil; electrify his brain with the lightnin' of the Word; put perpetual motion in his arms; fill him plumb full of dynamite of Thy glory; anoint him all over with the kerosene of salvation, and set him on fire. Amen!"

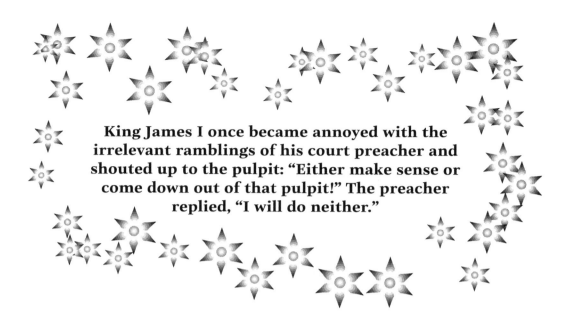

King James I once became annoyed with the irrelevant ramblings of his court preacher and shouted up to the pulpit: "Either make sense or come down out of that pulpit!" The preacher replied, "I will do neither."

A woman approached the minister after the sermon, and thanked him for his talk. "I found it so helpful," she said.

The minister replied: "I hope it will not prove as helpful as the last sermon you heard me preach."

"Why, what do you mean?" asked the astonished woman.

"Well," said the minister, "that sermon lasted you three months."

A man is stumbling through the woods totally drunk when he comes upon a preacher baptising people in the river. He proceeds to walk into the water and subsequently bumps into the preacher.

The preacher turns around and is almost overcome by the smell of alcohol. Whereupon he asks the drunk, "Are you ready to find Jesus?"

The drunk answers, "Yes, I am."

So the preacher grabs him and dunks him in the water. He pulls him up and asks the drunk, "Brother, have you found Jesus?"

The drunk tells him, "No, I haven't found Jesus."

The preacher, shocked at the answer, dunks him into the water again for a little longer this time. He again pulls him out of the water and asks again, "Have you found Jesus, my brother?"

The drunk again answers, "No, I haven't found Jesus."

By this time the preacher is at his wits' end and dunks the drunk in the water again – but this time holds him down for about 30 seconds and when he begins kicking his arms and legs he pulls him up. The preacher again asks the drunk, "For the love of God, have you found Jesus?"

The drunk wipes his eyes and catches his breath and says to the preacher, "Are you sure this is where he fell in?"

One minister never prepared during the week, and on Sunday morning he'd sit on the platform while the church was singing the hymns desperately praying, "Lord, give me your message, Lord give me your message." One Sunday, while desperately praying for God's message, he heard the Lord say, "Derek, here's my message. You're lazy!"

The Revd Dr Robert South, while preaching one day in 1689, looked up from his notes to observe that his entire congregation was fast asleep – including the King! Appropriately mortified by this discovery, he interrupted his sermon to call out, "Lord Lauderdale, rouse yourself. You snore so loudly that you will wake the King."

Mark Twain attended a Sunday morning sermon. He met the pastor at the door afterwards and told him that he had a book at home with every word he had preached that morning. The minister assured him that the sermon was an original. Twain still held his position. The pastor wanted to see this book so Twain said he would send it over in the morning. When the preacher unwrapped it he found a dictionary and in the flyleaf was written this: "Words, just words, just words."

Proverbs

The following ten statements are long-winded versions of great proverbs. Can you tell what they are?

1. Fix something right away or it will get worse.
2. An over-abundance of culinary help is detrimental to the pot's contents.
3. Just because something is shiny, doesn't mean it's a precious metal.
4. That which pleases the eye doesn't go beyond the epidermis.
5. The capital of Italy was constructed over a long period of time.
6. There comes a time when your canine friend is through studying.
7. If you're going to give advice to others, be sure you follow it yourself.
8. Just because you aren't punctual doesn't mean you should quit.
9. If you never try to do anything, you'll never get anything done.
10. It doesn't take long for a person without good sense to be separated from his financial assets!

Answers:

1. A stitch in time saves nine.
2. Too many cooks spoil the broth.
3. All that glitters is not gold.
4. Beauty is only skin deep.
5. Rome wasn't built in a day.
6. You can't teach an old dog new tricks.
7. Practice what you preach.
8. Better late than never.
9. Nothing ventured, nothing gained.
10. A fool and his money are soon parted.

Provision

Moses and the people were in the desert, but what was he going to do with them? They had to be fed, and feeding 2 or 3 million people requires a lot of food. According to the Quartermaster General in the Army, it is reported that Moses would have to have had 1,500 tons of food each day. Do you know that to bring that much food each day, two freight trains, each at least a mile long, would be required?

Besides you must remember, they were out in the desert, so they would have to have firewood to use in cooking the food. This would take 4,000 tons of wood and a few more freight trains, each a mile long, just for one day.

And just think, they were 40 years in transit.

And, oh yes, they would have to have water. If they only had enough to drink and wash a few dishes, it would take 11,000,000 gallons each day and a freight train with tank cars, 1,800 miles long, just to bring water!

And then another thing! They had to get across the Red Sea at night. Now, if they went on a narrow path, double file, the line would be 800 miles long and would require 35 days and nights to get through. So there had to be a space in the Red Sea, three miles wide so that they could walk 5,000 abreast to get over in one night.

But then, there is another problem…each time they camped at the end of the day, a campsite two-thirds the size of the state of Rhode Island was required, or a total of 750 square miles…think of it! This much space for camping.

Do you think Moses figured all this out before he left Egypt? I think not!

You see, Moses believed in God. God took care of these things for him.

Where God guides, he provides!

When God gives the vision, he gives the provision.

Quality

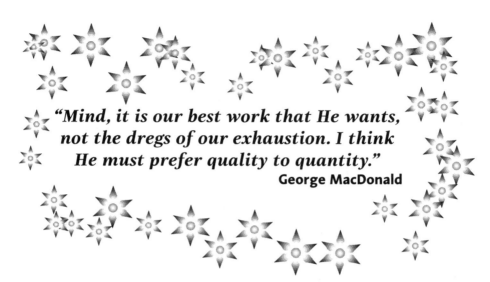

"Mind, it is our best work that He wants, not the dregs of our exhaustion. I think He must prefer quality to quantity."
George MacDonald

Questions

A friend once asked Isidor I Rabi, a Nobel prize winner in science, how he became a scientist. Rabi replied that every day after school his mother would talk to him about his school day. She wasn't so much interested in what he had learned that day, but she always inquired, "Did you ask a good question today?"

"Asking good questions," Rabi said, "made me become a scientist."

If you never felt pain, how would you know that I'm a Healer?

If you never went through difficulty, how would you know that I'm a Deliverer?

If you never had a trial, how would you know that I'm a Comforter?

If you never made a mistake, how would you know that I'm Forgiving?

If you know it all, how would you know that I will answer your questions?

If you never were in trouble, how would you know that I will come to your rescue?

If you never were broken, how would you know that I can make you whole?

If you never had a problem, then how would you know that I can solve them?

If you never had known suffering, then how would you know what I went through?

If you never went through the fire, then how would you become pure?

Quiet Times

The first hour of the morning is the rudder of the day.
Henry Ward Beecher

"Every now and then go away, have a little relaxation, for when you come back to your work your judgment will be surer, since to remain constantly at work will cause you to lose power of judgment... Go some distance away because then the work appears smaller, and more of it can be taken in at a glance, and lack of harmony or proportion is more readily seen."

Leonardo da Vinci

R

Reading

A minister with failing eyesight glanced at the note that Mrs Jones had sent to him by an usher.

The note read: "Bill Jones having gone to sea, his wife desires the prayers of the congregation for his safety."

Failing to observe the punctuation, he startled his audience by announcing:

"Bill Jones, having gone to see his wife, desires the prayers of the congregation for his safety."

Reconciliation

One New Year's Eve at London's Garrick Club, British dramatist Frederick Lonsdale was asked by Seymour Hicks to be reconciled with a fellow member. The two had quarrelled in the past and never restored their friendship. "You must," Hicks said to Lonsdale. "It is very unkind to be unfriendly at such a time. Go over now and wish him a happy New Year."

So Lonsdale crossed the room and spoke to his enemy. "I wish you a happy New Year," he said, "but only one."

Two brothers who lived on adjoining farms once fell into conflict. It was the first serious rift in 40 years of farming side by side, sharing machinery, and trading labour and goods as needed without a hitch. Then the long collaboration fell apart. It began with a small misunderstanding and it grew into a major difference, and finally it exploded into an exchange of bitter words followed by weeks of silence.

One morning there was a knock on John's door. He opened it to find a man with a carpenter's toolbox. "I'm looking for a few days work," he said. "Perhaps you would have a few small jobs here and there. Could I help you?"

"Yes," said the elder brother. "I do have a job for you. Look across the creek at that farm. That's my neighbour, in fact, it's my younger brother. Last week there was a meadow between us and he took his bulldozer to the river bank and now there is a creek between us. Well, he may have done this to spite me, but I'll go him one better. See that pile of lumber curing by the barn? I want you to build me a fence – an eight-foot fence – so I won't need to see his place anymore. Cool him down, anyhow."

The carpenter said, "I think I understand the situation. Show me the nails and the post-hole digger and I'll be able to do a job that pleases you."

The elder brother had to go to town for supplies, so he helped the carpenter get the materials ready and then he was off for the day. The carpenter worked hard all that day measuring, sawing, nailing.

About sunset when the farmer returned, the carpenter had just finished his job. The farmer's eyes opened wide, his jaw dropped.

There was no fence there at all. It was a bridge – a bridge stretching from one side of the creek to the other! A fine piece of work, handrails and all – and the neighbour, his younger brother, was coming across, his hand outstretched. "You are quite a fellow to build this bridge after all I've said and done."

The two brothers met at the middle of the bridge, taking each other's hand. They turned to see the carpenter hoist his toolbox on his shoulder. "No, wait! Stay a few days. I've a lot of other projects for you," said the elder brother. "I'd love to stay on," the carpenter said, "but I have so many more bridges to build."

Relevance

The elderly priest, speaking to the younger priest, said, "It was a good idea to replace the first four pews with plush theatre seats. It worked. The front of the church fills first."

The young priest nodded and the old one continued,

"And you told me a little more beat to the music would bring young people back to church, so I supported you when you brought in that rock 'n roll gospel choir. We are packed to the balcony."

"Thank you, Father," answered the young priest, "I am pleased you are open to the new ideas of youth."

"However," said the elderly priest, "I'm afraid you've gone too far with the drive-thru Confessional."

"But Father," protested the young priest. "My confessions have nearly doubled since I began that!"

"I know, son," replied the old man. "But that flashing neon sign, 'Toot 'n Tell or Go to Hell', is just not staying on the church roof."

S

Sacrifice

Obituary in The Times, *September 2002*

Necdet Kent
1911–2002

Necdet Kent, who has died aged 91, risked his life to save 80 Jews from the concentration camps during World War II.

In 1943 Kent was the Turkish consul-general in Marseilles, France. One evening, he heard rumours that Turkish Jews living in the city were being rounded up by the Gestapo and loaded into cattle trucks. Immediately, Kent rushed to the station, where he found 80 people crammed into wagons, bound for Germany and certain death. "To this day," he said a few years ago, "I remember the inscription on one of the wagons: 'This wagon may be loaded with 20 heads of cattle and 500kg of grass'." When Kent demanded the release of his countrymen, he was told by the Gestapo commander that these were "not Turks or anything of the sort, but just plain Jews".

At this point, Kent realised there was only one possible course of action: he pushed the officer aside, and boarded the train himself. "Now it was the Gestapo officer's turn to do the begging. I didn't respond to anything that was said, and the train began to move."

At the next station, he was met by Gestapo officers who apologised for the fact that the train had left Marseilles before letting him disembark, and explained that a car was waiting to take him back. But Kent was immovable. "I explained that more than 80 Turkish citizens had been loaded on to these animal wagons because they were Jews, and that I was a representative of a government that rejected such treatment." Dumbfounded by his audacity, the Germans let everyone off the train. The Jews, who were sent to safety in Istanbul for the duration of the war, flung their arms around Kent in relief and gratitude. "I cannot forget those embraces," he said. "The inner peace I felt when I reached my bed towards morning that day is one I have not savoured much since."

He later saved many more Jews by issuing them with Turkish papers.

In 2001 Kent was presented with a special medal from Israel bearing the legend: "Saving one life is like saving all the world".

He said at the ceremony: "What I have done is what I should have done. I knew I had to act."

In the fourth century AD in Korea a man had two sons. The elder rose to become Chief Justice in the land and the younger became an infamous bandit.

The elder brother loved his younger brother but was unable to persuade him to change his ways.

Eventually the younger son was caught and brought before his brother, the Chief Justice. Everyone in the courtroom thought the younger brother would get off because it was well known that the Chief Justice loved his brother.

But at the end of the trial, the Chief Justice sentenced his brother to death.

On the day of the execution, the elder brother came to the prison and said to his brother, "Let's swap places." The younger brother agreed thinking that once they realised that it was the elder brother, the execution would not go forward.

On he went up the hill to watch proceedings. His brother was brought out at dawn, and, to his horror, executed.

Filled with remorse, he ran down the hill and told the guard his name and that he was the criminal who should be executed. The guards said to him:

"There is no sentence outstanding on anyone with that name."

During the 17th century, Oliver Cromwell, Lord Protector of England, sentenced a soldier to be shot for his crimes. The execution was to take place at the ringing of the evening curfew bell. However, the bell did not sound. The soldier's fiancée had climbed into the belfry and clung to the great clapper of the bell to prevent it from striking. When she was summoned by Cromwell to account for her actions, she wept as she showed him her bruised and bleeding hands. Cromwell's heart was touched and he said, "Your lover shall live because of your sacrifice. Curfew shall not ring tonight!"

Salvation

A minister was working late one Saturday night, and decided to call his wife before he left for home. It was about 10:00pm, but his wife didn't answer the phone.

The minister let it ring many times. He thought it was odd that she didn't answer, but decided to wrap up a few things and try again in a few minutes.

When he tried again she answered right away. He asked her why she hadn't answered before, and she said that it hadn't rung at their house. They brushed it off as a fluke and forgot about the matter.

The following Monday, the minister received a call at the church office, which was the phone that he'd used that Saturday night. The man he spoke with wanted to know why he'd called on Saturday night. The minister couldn't figure out what the man was talking about.

Then the man said, "It rang and rang, but I didn't answer." The minister remembered the mishap and apologised for disturbing him, explaining that he'd intended to call his wife. The man said, "That's OK. Let me tell you my story. You see, I was planning to commit suicide on Saturday night, but before I did, I prayed, 'God if you're there, and you don't want me to do this, give me a sign now.' At that point my phone started to ring. I looked at the caller ID, and it said, 'Almighty God'. I was afraid to answer!"

The reason why it showed on the man's caller ID that the call came from "Almighty God" is because the church that the minister attends is called Almighty God Tabernacle.

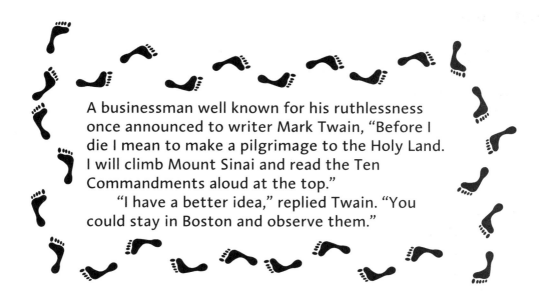

A businessman well known for his ruthlessness once announced to writer Mark Twain, "Before I die I mean to make a pilgrimage to the Holy Land. I will climb Mount Sinai and read the Ten Commandments aloud at the top."

"I have a better idea," replied Twain. "You could stay in Boston and observe them."

When the author walks onto the stage, the play is over. God is going to invade, all right; but what is the good of saying you are on His side then, when you see the whole natural universe melting away like a dream and something else comes crashing in? This time it will be God without disguise; something so overwhelming that it will strike either irresistible love or irresistible horror into every creature. It will be too late then to choose your side. That will not be the time for choosing; it will be the time when we discover which side we really have chosen, whether we realised it before or not. Now, today, this moment, is our chance to choose the right side.

C S Lewis

Science

A group of scientists got together and decided that man had come a long way and no longer needed God. They picked one scientist to go and tell God that they no longer needed Him.

God listened patiently and kindly to the man and after the scientist finished, God said, "Very well! How about this? Let's have a man-making contest."

To which the man replied, "OK, great!"

But God added, "Now we're going to do this just like I did back in the old days with Adam."

The scientist said, "Sure, no problem" and bent down and grabbed a handful of dirt.

God just looked at him and said, "No, no, no. You make your own dirt!"

Service

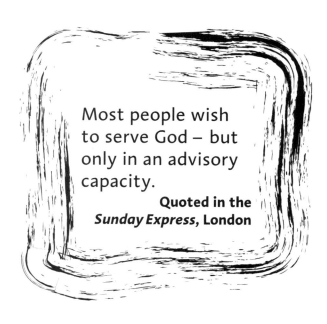

Most people wish to serve God – but only in an advisory capacity.

Quoted in the
Sunday Express, **London**

Years ago, the Salvation Army was holding an international convention and their founder, General William Booth, could not attend because of physical weakness. He cabled his convention message to them. It was one word: "OTHERS".

Dave Thomas, founder of Wendy's Hamburgers is the only founder among America's big companies whose picture in the corporate annual report shows him wielding a mop and a plastic bucket. That wasn't a gag either, it was done intentionally so that he could lead by example. At Wendy's an MBA does not mean a "Master of Business Administration", it means "Mop Bucket Attitude!" Service at the lowest levels makes for great success.

Sex

The vicar decided to do something a little different one Sunday morning. He said, "Today, I am going to say a single word and you are going to help me preach. Whatever single word I say, I want you to sing whatever hymn that comes to your mind."

So he shouted out CROSS. Immediately, the congregation started singing in unison THE OLD RUGGED CROSS.

He shouted out GRACE. The congregation began to sing AMAZING GRACE.

He said POWER. The congregation sang THERE IS POWER IN THE BLOOD.

The vicar finally said SEX. The congregation fell in total silence. Everyone was in shock. They all nervously began to look around at each other afraid to say anything.

Then all of a sudden, from way back in the church, a little 88-year-old grandmother stood up and began to sing MEMORIES.

Signs

On a plumber's truck: "WE REPAIR WHAT YOUR HUSBAND FIXED."

A plumbing company: "DON'T SLEEP WITH A DRIP. CALL YOUR PLUMBER."

In a vet's waiting room: "BE BACK IN FIVE MINUTES. SIT! STAY!"

Door of a plastic surgeon's office: "WE CAN HELP YOU PICK YOUR NOSE!"

On an electrician's van: "LET US REMOVE YOUR SHORTS."

In a non-smoking area: "IF WE SEE SMOKE, WE WILL ASSUME YOU ARE ON FIRE AND TAKE APPROPRIATE ACTION."

On a maternity room door: "PUSH. PUSH. PUSH."

At an optometrist's office: "IF YOU DON'T SEE WHAT YOU'RE LOOKING FOR, YOU'VE COME TO THE RIGHT PLACE."

In a toilet in a London office block: "TOILET OUT OF ORDER. PLEASE USE FLOOR BELOW."

Outside a second-hand shop: "WE EXCHANGE ANYTHING – BICYCLES, WASHING MACHINES ETC. WHY NOT BRING YOUR WIFE ALONG AND GET A WONDERFUL BARGAIN?"

Sign on a repair shop door: "WE CAN REPAIR ANYTHING. (PLEASE KNOCK HARD ON THE DOOR – THE BELL DOESN'T WORK)."

Sign in a laundrette: "AUTOMATIC WASHING MACHINES: PLEASE REMOVE ALL YOUR CLOTHES WHEN THE LIGHT GOES OUT."

Sign in a London department store: "BARGAIN BASEMENT UPSTAIRS."

In an office: "WOULD THE PERSON WHO TOOK THE STEP LADDER YESTERDAY PLEASE BRING IT BACK OR FURTHER STEPS WILL BE TAKEN."

Outside a photographer's studio: "OUT TO LUNCH: IF NOT BACK BY FIVE, OUT FOR DINNER ALSO."

Outside a disco: "SMARTS IS THE MOST EXCLUSIVE DISCO IN TOWN… EVERYONE WELCOME."

Sign warning of quicksand: "QUICKSAND. ANY PERSON PASSING THIS POINT WILL BE DROWNED. BY ORDER OF THE DISTRICT COUNCIL."

Notice in a dry cleaner's window: "ANYONE LEAVING THEIR GARMENTS HERE FOR MORE THAN 30 DAYS WILL BE DISPOSED OF."

Sign on motorway garage: "PLEASE DO NOT SMOKE NEAR OUR PETROL PUMPS… YOUR LIFE MAY NOT BE WORTH MUCH, BUT OUR PETROL IS."

Notice in health food shop window: "CLOSED DUE TO ILLNESS."

Signs (outside church)

God does not go on a vacation from you.

If you live as if God doesn't exist, you better be right!

The Nails Didn't Keep Jesus On The Cross –
His Love For You Did.

Professionals Built The Titanic.
Amateurs Built The Ark.

Always plan ahead! It didn't rain when Noah built the ark.

The Ten Commandments were NOT called The Ten Suggestions.

If you don't fellowship, you are not among the fellow sheep.

Tough week? We are open Sundays.

Does your Spiritual house need spring cleaning?

Our world revolves around the Son.

Even through the storm, the Son still shines.

Free trip to Heaven. Details inside.

Need directions? I've got them. God

If God is your co-pilot...SWAP SEATS!

You thought Mr Clean took out dirt? TRY JESUS!

Be as patient with others as God has been with you.

Give your troubles to God. He's up all night anyway.

**STOMACH ACHE? – Doctor
TOOTH ACHE? – Dentist
HEART ACHE? – God**

The Bible is your best TV Guide.

Prayer gives you a calm-plex.

Feeling let down today? Try looking up.

T.G.I.F. – Thank God I'm Forgiven.

Jesus invested His life in you. Have you shown any interest?

Get an afterlife.

My way is the High Way. God

Let's meet Sunday...face-to-faith. God

Will the road that you're travelling on get you to my place? God

Have you read my number one best seller?
There will be a test. God

It's never too soon to plan for eternity.

Do not wait for the hearse to take you to church.

If you're headed in the wrong direction, God allows U-turns.

If you don't like the way you were born, try being born again.

Forbidden fruit creates many jams.

In the dark? Follow the Son.

Running low on faith? Stop in for a fill-up.

If you can't sleep, don't count sheep. Talk to the Shepherd.

An ad for a church has a picture of two hands holding stone tablets on which the Ten Commandments are inscribed and a headline that reads, "For fast, fast, fast relief, take two tablets".

When the restaurant next to the Church put out a big sign with red letters that said, "Open Sundays", the church reciprocated with its own message: "We are open on Sundays, too."

Sin

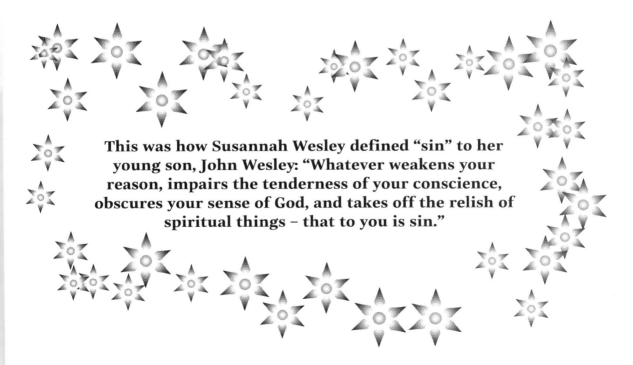

This was how Susannah Wesley defined "sin" to her young son, John Wesley: "Whatever weakens your reason, impairs the tenderness of your conscience, obscures your sense of God, and takes off the relish of spiritual things – that to you is sin."

I live in a small, rural community. There are lots of cattle ranches around here, and, every once in a while, a cow wanders off and gets lost... Ask a rancher how a cow gets lost, and chances are he will reply, "Well, the cow starts nibbling on a tuft of green grass, and when it finishes, it looks ahead to the next tuft of green grass and starts nibbling on that one, and then it nibbles on a tuft of grass right next to a hole in the fence. It then sees another tuft of green grass on the other side of the fence, so it nibbles on that one and then goes on to the next tuft. The next thing you know, the cow has nibbled itself into being lost."

People are in the process of nibbling their way to being lost... We keep moving from one tuft of activity to another, never noticing how far we have gone from home or how far away from the truth we have managed to end up.

Mike Yaconelli

"A little sin is like being a little pregnant. It will eventually show itself."
Rick Warren

Once we assuage our conscience by calling something a "necessary evil", it begins to look more and more necessary and less and less evil.
Sidney J Harris

Sin arises when things that are a minor good are pursued as though they were the most important goals in life. If money or affection or power are sought in disproportionate, obsessive ways, then sin occurs. And that sin is magnified when, for these lesser goals, we fail to pursue the highest good and the finest goals. So when we ask ourselves why, in a given situation, we committed a sin, the answer is usually one of two things. Either we wanted to obtain something we didn't have, or we feared losing something we had.

St Augustine

When John Belushi died in the spring of 1983 from an overdose of cocaine and heroin, a variety of articles appeared, including one in *US News and World Report*, on the seductive dangers of cocaine: "It can do you no harm and it can drive you insane; it can give you status in society and it can wreck your career; it can make you the life of the party and it can turn you into a loner; it can be an elixir for high living and a potion for death."

Like all sin, there's a difference between the appearance and the reality, between the momentary feeling and the lasting effect.

Singing

A CHOIR PROFICIENCY TEST

In order to measure your level of proficiency as a choir member, the following test has been carefully developed by experts. Read each situation and then select the option that will enhance the quality of your performance.

1. You are a soprano and count incorrectly. As a result you boom out a high "C" one measure too soon. You should:
   a. Slide into an inspired "O for a thousand tongues to sing".
   b. Look triumphant and hold on to the note.
   c. Stop abruptly in mid squawk but keep your lips moving.
   d. Sink to the floor in shame.

2. After all those long hard choir rehearsals, you show up 20 minutes late for the Christmas musical. You should:
   a. Climb into the back row of the choir from the baptistry.
   b. Enter pretending to be a sound man checking cables and then suddenly slip yourself into the choir.
   c. Turn the lights out in the church and slip into the choir during the blackout.
   d. Read M Stephen's book, *Techniques for Tardy Appearances*.

3. While singing, you discover you have only one page of a two-page hymn. You should:
   a. Hum for your life.
   b. Sing "Watermelon, watermelon, watermelon".
   c. Try to get another hymnal out of the choir rack with your feet.
   d. Sing the first page over again.

4. Inevitably that dreaded big sneeze occurs toward the end of the choir special. You should:
   a. As you sneeze, come down hard on your neighbour's foot to create a diversion.
   b. Try to make it harmonise.
   c. Sneeze into the hair of the choir member in front of you to muffle the noise.
   d. Sink to the floor in shame.

Count the number of As, Bs, Cs, and Ds you checked and find your proficiency rating below:

3 or more As...there is nothing more you need to know to be a first-rate choir member.

3 or more Bs...your church choir reflexes are fully developed and you should do well in choir.

3 or more Cs...your church choral experience is spotty but your team spirit is on target. You will be an asset to any choir.

3 or more Ds...it is recommended you take up personal fitness classes or group therapy counselling.

Sisters

Andrew came home from school one day, cut, bruised and blood stained. His father asked him what on earth had happened.

"Well, Dad, it's like this," Andrew began. "Stephen challenged me to a duel and you know how that goes... we have a choice of weapons."

"Uh huh," said his father. "That seems fair."

"I know... but I never thought he'd choose his sister!"

Smile

Holiday Inn, when looking for 500 people to fill positions for a new facility, interviewed 5,000 candidates. The hotel managers interviewing these people excluded all candidates who smiled fewer than four times during the interview. This applied to people competing for jobs in all categories.

Soul

Once upon a time there was a rich King who had four wives.

He loved the fourth wife the most and adorned her with rich robes and treated her to the finest of delicacies. He gave her nothing but the best.

He also loved the third wife very much and was always showing her off to neighbouring kingdoms. However, he feared that one day she would leave him for another.

He also loved his second wife. She was his confidante and was always kind, considerate and patient with him. Whenever the King faced a problem, he could confide in her, and she would help him get through the difficult times.

The King's first wife was a very loyal partner and had made great contributions in maintaining his wealth and kingdom. However, he did not love the first wife. Although she loved him deeply, he hardly took notice of her.

One day, the King fell ill and he knew his time was short. He thought of his luxurious life and wondered, "I now have four wives with me, but when I die, I'll be all alone."

Thus, he asked the fourth wife, "I have loved you the most, endowed you with the finest clothing and showered great care over you. Now that I'm dying, will you follow me and keep me company?"

"No way!" replied the fourth wife, and she walked away without another word. Her answer cut like a sharp knife right into his heart.

The sad King then asked the third wife, "I have loved you all my life. Now that I'm dying, will you follow me and keep me company?"

"No!" replied the third wife. "Life is too good! When you die, I'm going to remarry!" His heart sank and turned cold.

He then asked the second wife, "I have always turned to you for help and you've always been there for me. When I die, will you follow me and keep me company?"

"I'm sorry, I can't help you out this time!" replied the second wife. "At the very most, I can only send you to your grave." Her answer came like a bolt of lightning, and the King was devastated.

Then a voice called out: "I'll leave with you and follow you no matter where you go." The King looked up, and there was his first wife. She was skinny because she had suffered from malnutrition and neglect.

Greatly grieved, the King said, "I should have taken much better care of you when I had the chance!"

In truth, we all have four wives in our lives:

Our fourth wife is our body. No matter how much time and effort we lavish in making it look good, it will leave us when we die.

Our third wife represents our possessions, status and wealth. When we die, they will all go to others.

Our second wife is our family and friends. No matter how much they have been there for us, the furthest they can stay by us is up to the grave.

And our first wife is our Soul which is often neglected in pursuit of wealth, power and pleasures of the world. However, our Soul is the only thing that will follow us wherever we go.

So cultivate, strengthen and cherish it now, for it is the only part of us that will follow us to the throne of God and continue with us throughout Eternity.

Suffering

The only monument in the world built in the shape of a bug – to honour a bug – is located in Fort Rucker, Alabama. In 1915 the Mexican boll weevil invaded southeast Alabama and destroyed 60% of the cotton crop. In desperation, the farmers turned to planting peanuts. By 1917 the peanut industry had become so profitable that the county harvested more peanuts than any other county in the nation. In gratitude, the people of the town erected a statue and inscribed these words,

"In profound appreciation of the boll weevil, and what it has done as the herald of prosperity".

The instrument of their suffering had become the means of their blessing.

In the frigid waters around Greenland are countless icebergs, some little and some gigantic. If you observe them carefully, you notice that sometimes the small ice floes move in one direction while their massive counterparts flow in another.

The explanation is simple. Surface winds drive the little ones, whereas the huge masses of ice are carried along by deep ocean currents. When we face trials and tragedies, it's helpful to see our lives as being subject to two forces – surface winds and ocean currents. The winds represent everything changeable, unpredictable, and distressing. But operating simultaneously with these gusts and gales is another force that's even more powerful. It is the sure movement of God's wise and sovereign purposes, the deep flow of His unchanging love.

I have in my hands two boxes
Which God gave me to hold
He said, "Put all your sorrows in the black,
And all your joys in the gold."
I heeded His words, and in the two boxes
Both my joys and sorrows I store
But though the gold became heavier each day
The black was as light as before.
With curiosity, I opened the black
I wanted to find out why
And I saw, in the base of the box, a hole
Which my sorrows had fallen out by.
I showed the hole to God, and mused aloud,
"I wonder where my sorrows could be."
He smiled a gentle smile at me.
"My child, they're all here with me."
I asked, "God, why give me the boxes,
Why the gold, and the black with the hole?"
"My child, the gold is for you to count your blessings,
the black is for you to let go."

T

Temptation

A newly married sailor was informed by the Navy that he was going to be stationed for a year a long way from home on a remote island in the Pacific. A few days after he got there he really began to miss his new wife, so he wrote her a letter.

"My love," he wrote, "we are going to be apart for a very long time. Already I'm starting to miss you and there's not much to do here in the evenings. Besides that, we're constantly surrounded by young attractive native girls. Do you think if I had a hobby of some kind I would not be tempted?"

So his wife sent him back a harmonica saying, "Why don't you learn to play this?"

Eventually his tour of duty came to an end and he rushed back to his wife. "Darling," he said, "I can't wait to see you for a cuddle!"

She kissed him, then said, "First, let's hear you play that harmonica."

All the water in the world
However hard it tries
Can never sink the smallest ship
Unless it gets inside

And all the evil in the world
The blackest kind of sin
Can never hurt you in the least
Unless you let it in

Anon

There is always free cheese in a mousetrap.

Thanksgiving

A Prayer of G K Chesterton

You say grace before meals.
All right.
But I say grace before the play and the opera,
And grace before the concert and the pantomime,
And grace before I open a book,
And grace before sketching, painting,
Swimming, fencing, boxing, walking, playing, dancing;
And grace before I dip the pen in the ink.

In Budapest, a man goes to the rabbi and complains, "Life is unbearable. There are nine of us living in one room. What can I do?"

The rabbi answers, "Take your goat into the room with you." The man in incredulous, but the rabbi insists. "Do as I say and come back in a week."

A week later the man comes back looking more distraught than before. "We cannot stand it," he tells the rabbi. "The goat is filthy."

The rabbi then tells him, "Go home and let the goat out. And come back in a week."

Radiant, the man returns to the rabbi a week later, exclaiming, "Life is beautiful. We enjoy every minute of it now that there's no goat — only the nine of us."

Although things are not perfect
Because of trial or pain
Continue in thanksgiving
Do not begin to blame
Even when the times are hard
Fierce winds are bound to blow
God is forever able
Hold on to what you know
Imagine life without His love
Joy would cease to be
Keep thanking Him for all the things
Love imparts to thee
Move out of "Camp Complaining"
No weapon that is known
On earth can yield the power
Praise can do alone
Quit looking at the future
Redeem the time at hand
Start every day with worship
To "thank" is a command
Until we see Him coming
Victorious in the sky
We'll run the race with gratitude
X alting God most high
Yes, there'll be good times and yes, some will be bad,

but...

Zion waits in glory...where none are ever sad!

Time

Time is a great teacher. Unfortunately it kills all its pupils.

What happened to Time?

- When as a child I laughed and wept, time crept.
- When as a youth I dreamed and talked, time walked.
- When I became a full-grown man, time ran.
- And later as I older grew, time flew.
- Soon I shall find while travelling on, time gone.

A unique way of keeping the time was discovered in Cape Town, South Africa. From the foot of Table Mountain a gun would be fired at noon. An observer watching the two gunners fire the cannon wondered how they could tell when to fire it, seeing as they had no radio. They pointed to a mounted telescope and replied that they could see a clock through it. The clock in question was outside a jeweller's shop and was declared to be the finest clock in the Cape.

Later in the day the observer found himself in town outside the jeweller's, so he went and asked the owner about the clock. The owner explained that it had been imported from Amsterdam in the 19th century and was the finest timekeeper in South Africa. When the observer asked the shopkeeper how he ensured that the clock was accurate each day, he replied that it was a relatively straightforward procedure. He set the clock by the sound of a noonday gun across the valley.

In a lifetime the average American will spend:

Six months sitting at stoplights
Eight months opening junk mail
One year looking for misplaced objects
Two years unsuccessfully returning
    phone calls
Four years doing housework
Five years waiting in line
Six years eating

Millions long for immortality who do not know what to do with themselves on a rainy Sunday afternoon.
Susan Ertz

i might pop up to Mick's cloud for a bit... wanna come?

nah

If you had a bank that credited your account each morning with £86,000, that carried over no balance from day to day, allowed you to keep no cash in your account, and every evening cancelled whatever part of the amount you failed to use during the day, what would you do?

Draw out every pound every day, of course, and use it to your advantage!

Well, you have such a bank, and its name is TIME! Every morning it credits you with 86,000 seconds. Every night it rules off as lost whatever of this you failed to invest to good purpose. It carries over no balances, it allows no overdrafts. Each day it opens a new account with you. If you fail to use the day's deposits, the loss is yours. There is no going back. There is no drawing against tomorrow.

The great 19th century naturalist and Harvard professor Louis Agassiz was once approached by the emissary of a learned society and invited to address its members. Agassiz declined the invitation, saying that lectures of this kind took up too much time that should be devoted to research and writing. The man persisted, saying that the society was prepared to pay handsomely for the lecture.

"That's no inducement to me," Agassiz replied, "I can't afford to waste my time making money."

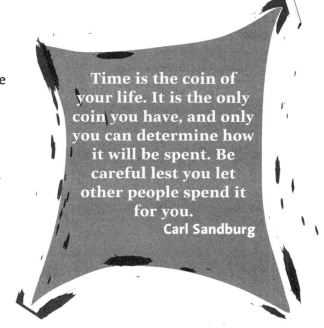

Time is the coin of your life. It is the only coin you have, and only you can determine how it will be spent. Be careful lest you let other people spend it for you.
Carl Sandburg

Transformation

The Nobel Peace Prize is the supreme award given to those who have made an exceptional contribution to the betterment of the world. Other Nobel Prizes are given to those who have made outstanding contributions in the arts and sciences. There is a story about a Nobel Prize that is rarely ever told.

Alfred Nobel, a Swedish chemist, made his fortune by inventing powerful explosives and licensing the formula to governments to make weapons. One day Nobel's brother died, and a newspaper by accident printed an obituary notice for Alfred instead of the deceased brother.

It identified him as the inventor of dynamite who made a fortune by enabling armies to achieve new levels of mass destruction. Nobel had the unique opportunity to read his own obituary in his lifetime and to see how he would be remembered. He was shocked to think that this was what his life would add up to: he would be remembered as a merchant of death and destruction.

He took his fortune and used it to establish the awards for accomplishments contributing to life rather than death. And today, Nobel indeed is remembered for his contribution to peace and human achievement – not explosives.

In 1921 Lewis Lawes became the warden at Sing Sing Prison. No prison was tougher than Sing Sing during that time. But when Warden Lawes retired some 20 years later, that prison had become a humanitarian institution. Those who studied the system said credit for the change belonged to Lawes. But when he was asked about the transformation, here's what he said: "I owe it all to my wonderful wife, Catherine, who is buried outside the prison walls."

Catherine Lawes was a young mother with three small children when her husband became the warden. Everybody warned her from the beginning that she should never set foot inside the prison walls, but that didn't stop Catherine! When the first prison basketball game was held, she went…walking into the gym with her three beautiful kids and she sat in the stands with the inmates. Her attitude was: "My husband and I are going to take care of these men and I believe they will take care of me! I don't have to worry."

She insisted on getting acquainted with them and their records. She discovered one convicted murderer was blind so she paid him a visit. Holding his hand in hers she said, "Do you read Braille?"

"What's Braille?" he asked. Then she taught him how to read. Years later he would weep in love for her.

Later, Catherine found a deaf-mute in prison. She went to school to learn how to use sign language. Many said that Catherine Lawes was the presence of Jesus that came alive again in Sing Sing from 1921 to 1937.

Then, she was killed in a car accident. The next morning Lewis Lawes didn't come to work, so the acting warden took his place. It seemed almost instantly that the prison knew something was wrong.

The following day, her body was resting in a casket in her home, three-quarters of a mile from the prison. As the acting warden took his early morning walk he was shocked to see a large crowd of the toughest, hardest-looking criminals gathered like a herd of animals at the main gate. He came closer and noted tears of grief and sadness. He knew how much they loved Catherine. He turned and faced the men, "All right, men, you can go. Just be sure and check in tonight!" Then he opened the gate and a parade of criminals walked, without a guard, the three-quarters of a mile to stand in line to pay their final respects to Catherine Lawes. And every one of them checked back in. Every one!

Tim Kimmel

Truth

"A lie gets half way round the world, before the truth has a chance to get its pants on."

Winston Churchill

The trouble with stretching the truth is that it's apt to snap back.

"Truth stands the test of time."
The Bible, Proverbs 12:19

The truth is always the strongest argument.

Greek proverb

Those that think it permissible to tell white lies soon grow colour blind.
Austin O'Malley

Henry Augustus Rowland, professor of physics at Johns Hopkins University, was once called as an expert witness at a trial. During cross-examination a lawyer demanded, "What are your qualifications as an expert witness in this case?"

The normally modest and retiring professor replied quietly, "I am the greatest living expert on the subject under discussion." Later a friend well acquainted with Rowland's disposition expressed surprise at the professor's uncharacteristic answer. Rowland answered, "Well, what did you expect me to do? I was under oath."

Once, when a stubborn disputer seemed unconvinced, Abraham Lincoln said, "Well, let's see, how many legs has a cow?"

"Four, of course," came the reply disgustedly.

"That's right," agreed Lincoln. "Now suppose you call the cow's tail a leg; how many legs would the cow have?"

"Why, five, of course," was the confident reply.

"Now, that's where you're wrong," said Lincoln. "Calling a cow's tail a leg doesn't make it a leg."

Writing letters of recommendation can be hazardous – tell the truth and you might get sued if the contents are negative. Robert Thornton, a professor at Lehigh University, has a collection of "virtually litigation-proof" phrases called the Lexicon of Intentionally Ambiguous Recommendations, or LIAR.

Here are some examples:

- To describe an inept person – "I enthusiastically recommend this candidate with no qualifications whatsoever."

- To describe an ex-employee who had problems getting along with fellow workers – "I am pleased to say that this candidate is a former colleague of mine."

- To describe an unproductive candidate – "I can assure you that no person would be better for the job."

- To describe an applicant not worth consideration – "I would urge you to waste no time in making this candidate an offer of employment."

The great enemy of the truth is very often not the lie – deliberate, contrived, and dishonest – but the myth – persistent, persuasive and unrealistic.

John F Kennedy

Most writers regard truth as their most valuable possession, and therefore are most economical in its use.

Mark Twain

Everyone loves the truth, but not everyone tells it.

Yiddish proverb

Father: I want an explanation and I want the truth!

Son: Make up your mind, Dad. You can't have both!

U

Unity

In a Peanuts cartoon Lucy demanded that Linus change TV channels, threatening him with her fist if he didn't. "What makes you think you can walk right in here and take over?" asks Linus.

"These five fingers," says Lucy. "Individually they're nothing but when I curl them together like this into a single unit, they form a weapon that is terrible to behold."

"Which channel do you want?" asks Linus. Turning away, he looks at his fingers and says, "Why can't you guys get organised like that?"

Charles Schultz

The snowflake is one of nature's most fragile things, but just look at what they can do when they stick together.
Vesta Kelly

There can be union without unity: tie two cats together by their tails and throw them over a clothes-line.

Universe

To help us grasp the vastness of our galaxy, one scientist suggests we imagine a smooth glass surface. Shrink the sun from 865,000 miles in diameter to two feet and place it on the surface. Using this scale, Earth would be 220 paces out from the sun, and would be the size of a pea. Mars, the size of a pinhead, would be 108 paces beyond Earth. But to reach Neptune, you'd need to step off another 6,130 paces from Mars. By now you would be five miles from the sun – but there still wouldn't be room on the glass surface for Pluto! You would have to pace off 6,720 miles beyond Pluto to reach the nearest star. Yet this glass model represents only a tiny fraction of the universe.

Urgency

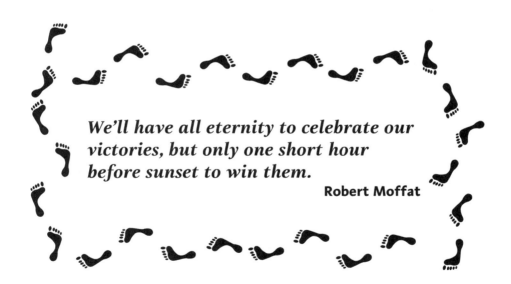

We'll have all eternity to celebrate our victories, but only one short hour before sunset to win them.
Robert Moffat

Valentines

After she woke up, a woman told her husband, "I just dreamed that you gave me a pearl necklace for Valentine's Day. What do you think it means?"

"You'll know tonight," he said.

That evening, the man came home with a small package and gave it to his wife. Delighted, she opened it – to find a book entitled "The Meaning of Dreams".

Value

A story is told of a man who loved old books. He met an acquaintance who had just thrown away a Bible that had been stored in the attic of his ancestral home for generations. "I couldn't read it," the friend explained. "Somebody named Guten-something had printed it."

"Not Gutenberg!" the book-lover exclaimed in horror. "That Bible was one of the first books ever printed. Why, a copy just sold for over two million dollars!" His friend was unimpressed. "Mine wouldn't have brought a dollar. Some fellow named Martin Luther had scribbled all over it in German."

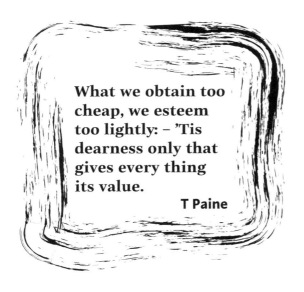

What we obtain too cheap, we esteem too lightly: – 'Tis dearness only that gives every thing its value.

T Paine

We know the cost of everything and the value of nothing.

Values

When actress Sophia Loren sobbed to Italian movie director Vittorio De Sica over the theft of her jewellery, he lectured her: "Listen to me, Sophia. I am much older than you and if there is one great truth I have learned about life, it is this – never cry over anything that can't cry over you."

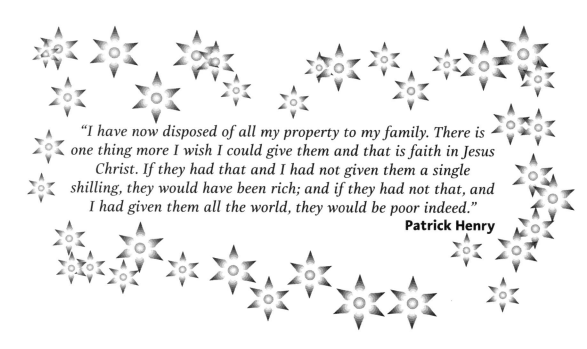

"I have now disposed of all my property to my family. There is one thing more I wish I could give them and that is faith in Jesus Christ. If they had that and I had not given them a single shilling, they would have been rich; and if they had not that, and I had given them all the world, they would be poor indeed."

Patrick Henry

Victory

There are no victories at discount prices.

General Dwight Eisenhower

Volunteers

On a blood-bank poster which read: "Be a volunteer Blood Donor", somebody had scrawled, "That's the best kind".

Wealth

There once was a rich man who was near death. He was very sad because he had worked so hard for his money and he wanted to be able to take it with him to Heaven. So he began to pray that he might be able to take some of his wealth with him.

An angel heard his plea and said to him, "Sorry, but you can't take your wealth with you."

The man implored the angel to speak to God to see if He might bend the rules. The man continued to pray that his wealth could follow him. The angel reappeared and informed the man that God had decided to allow him to take one suitcase with him. Overjoyed, the man gathered his largest suitcase and filled it with pure gold bars and placed it beside his bed.

Soon afterwards the man died and arrived at the Gates of Heaven to greet St Peter. St Peter, seeing the suitcase said, "Hold on, you can't bring that in here!"

But, the man explained to St Peter that he had permission and asked him to verify his story with the Lord. Sure enough, St Peter checked and came back saying, "You're right. You are allowed one carry-on bag, but I'm supposed to check its contents before letting it through."

St Peter opened the suitcase to inspect the worldly items that the man found too precious to leave behind and exclaimed, "You brought pavement?"

There was a man who had worked all his life and had saved all of his money. He was a real miser when it came to spending. He loved money more than anything, and as he was very ill, he said to his wife, "Now listen… when I die, I want you to take all my money and put it in the coffin with me."

And so he got his wife to promise him with all of her heart that when he died, she would comply with his wish.

Well, one day he died and his body was laid out in the coffin. The wife was sitting there in black, and her friend was sitting next to her.

When they had finished the ceremony, just as the undertakers got ready to close the lid, the wife said, "Wait just a minute!" She brought out a box and put it in the coffin next to the body.

The undertakers locked the coffin down, and rolled it away.

Her friend said, "Girl, I know you weren't fool enough to put all that money in there."

She said, "Listen, I'm a Christian, I promised him that I was going to put all his money in the coffin with him."

"You mean to tell me you put every penny in the coffin?"

"I certainly did," said the wife. "I wrote him a cheque."

Measure wealth not by the things you have,
but by the things you have for which you
would not take money.

Weddings

A man goes to a friend's wedding and is very impressed with the choice of hymns, especially "Love Divine". He is due to be married himself a few months later, so he makes a note of the number: 343.

When he next meets with the minister who is to conduct his wedding, he tells him he would like hymn 343.

"Are you sure?" asks the minister. "It is rather an unusual choice!"

"No, I am certain. I heard it at my friend's wedding, and it is just what I want to say," insists the man.

What he had not realised is that his friend was married in a Methodist church, using the Methodist Hymn Book, whereas at his wedding they were using Hymns Ancient and Modern.

Imagine the surprise of all – not least the bride – when they started to sing Hymns Ancient and Modern 343:

Come, O thou traveller unknown
whom still I hold, but cannot see;
my company before is gone
and I am left alone with thee;
With thee all night I mean to
    stay,
and wrestle till the break of day.

Work

"The hardest thing about milking cows," observed a farmer, "is that they never stay milked."

A manager and a sales rep stood looking at a map on which coloured pins indicated the company representative in each area. "I'm not going to fire you, Wilson," the manager said, "but I'm loosening your pin a bit just to emphasise the insecurity of your situation."

The Five Stages of a Project

Stage 1: Excitement, euphoria
Stage 2: Disenchantment
Stage 3: Search for the guilty
Stage 4: Punishment of the innocent
Stage 5: Distinction for the uninvolved

Nine workplace attitudes bosses hate:

NMJ – Not my job
NMM – Need more money
WCT – Wastes company time
PPP – Promises, promises, promises
NMH – Needs more help
ACD – Always complaining and disagreeable
CWS – Clock watcher's syndrome
TTM – The trouble maker
SRM – Supports rumour mill

The work of a Beethoven, and the work of a charwoman, become spiritual on precisely the same condition, that of being offered to God, of being done humbly "as to the Lord". This does not, of course, mean that it is for anyone a mere toss-up whether he should sweep rooms or compose symphonies. A mole must dig to the glory of God and a cock must crow.

C S Lewis

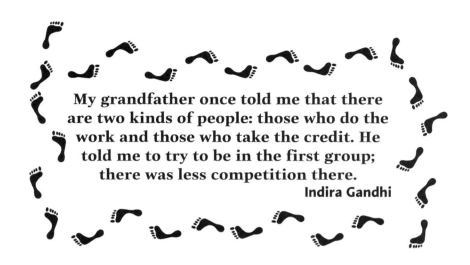

My grandfather once told me that there are two kinds of people: those who do the work and those who take the credit. He told me to try to be in the first group; there was less competition there.

Indira Gandhi

The "Coronary and Ulcer Club" lists the following rules for members:

1. Your job comes first. Forget everything else.
2. Saturdays, Sundays, and holidays are fine times to be working at the office. There will be nobody else there to bother you.
3. Always have your briefcase with you when not at your desk. This provides an opportunity to review completely all the troubles and worries of the day.
4. Never say "no" to a request. Always say "yes".
5. Accept all invitations to meetings, banquets, committees, etc.
6. All forms of recreation are a waste of time.
7. Never delegate responsibility to others; carry the entire load yourself.
8. If your work calls for travelling, work all day and travel at night to keep that appointment you made for eight the next morning.
9. No matter how many jobs you already are doing, remember you always can take on more.

Worry

For several years a woman had been having trouble getting to sleep at night because she feared burglars. One night her husband heard a noise in the house, so he went downstairs to investigate. When he got there, he did find a burglar. "Good evening," said the man of the house. "I am pleased to see you. Come upstairs and meet my wife. She has been waiting ten years to meet you."

The beginning of anxiety is the end of faith, and the beginning of true faith is the end of anxiety. George Muller Massena, one of Napoleon's generals, suddenly appeared with 18,000 soldiers before an Austrian town which had no means of defending itself. The town council met, certain that capitulation was the only answer. The old dean of the church reminded the council that it was Easter, and begged them to hold services as usual and to leave the trouble in God's hands. They followed his advice. The dean went to the church and rang the bells to announce the service. The French soldiers heard the church bells ring and concluded that the Austrian Army had come to rescue the town. They broke camp, and before the bells had ceased ringing, vanished.

J Arthur Rank, an English executive, decided to do all his worrying on one day each week. He chose Wednesdays. When anything happened that gave him anxiety and annoyed his ulcer, he would write it down and put it in his worry box and forget about it until next Wednesday. The interesting thing was that on the following Wednesday when he opened his worry box, he found that most of the things that had disturbed him during the past six days were already settled. It would have been useless to have worried about them.

X

X-Rays

The medical student was shocked when he received a fail in radiology. Approaching the professor, he demanded to know the reason for the grade.

"You know the self X-ray you took?" asked the professor.

"I do," said the student.

"A fine picture," the professor said, "of your lungs, stomach, and liver."

"If it's a fine picture, then why did you give me an F?" asked the student.

"I had no choice," said the professor.

"You didn't put your heart into it."

A young girl was told she needed an X-ray. She went in and seemed especially nervous.

When she came out of the X-ray room, she told her mother, "They took a picture of my bones."

"Yes, dear," replied her mother. "Did everything go all right?"

"Sure," said the girl. "It was great. I didn't even have to take my skin off!"

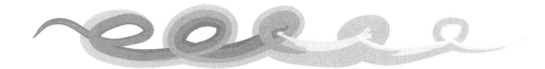

Y

Yielding

In the summer of 1986, two ships collided in the Black Sea off the coast of Russia. Hundreds of passengers died as they were hurled into the icy waters below. News of the disaster was further darkened when an investigation revealed the cause of the accident. It wasn't a technological problem like radar malfunction – or even thick fog. The cause was human stubbornness. Each captain was aware of the other ship's presence nearby. Both could have steered clear, but, according to news reports, neither captain wanted to give way to the other. Each was too proud to yield first. By the time they came to their senses, it was too late.

Youth

A renowned rabbi was travelling on a train. Three impudent youths decided to intimidate the Jew. They each made fun of the rabbi:

"Good morning, Father Abraham!"

"Good morning, Father Isaac!"

"Good morning, Father Jacob!"

But to their surprise, the rabbi replied:

"I am none of these. I am, however, Saul, the son of Kish, who was in a three-day search for the lost donkeys, and I'm glad I've finally found them!"

A Teenager is...

A person who can't remember to walk the dog but never forgets a phone number.

A youngster who receives their allowance on Monday, spends it on Tuesday, and borrows from their best friend on Wednesday.

Someone who can hear a song by Madonna played three blocks away but not his mother calling from the next room.

A whiz kid who can operate the latest computer without a lesson but can't make a bed.

A student who will spend twelve minutes studying for her history exam and twelve hours for her driver's licence.

A youngster who is well informed about anything he doesn't have to study.

An enthusiast who has the energy to ride a bike for miles, but is usually too tired to dry the dishes.

A connoisseur of two kinds of fine music: Loud and Very Loud.

A young woman who loves the cat and tolerates her brother.

A person who is always late for dinner but always on time for a rock concert.

A boy who can sleep until noon on any Saturday when he suspects the lawn needs mowing.

An original thinker who is positive that her mother was never a teenager.

For all of you with teenagers you may want to know why they really have a lot in common with cats:

1. Neither teenagers nor cats turn their heads when you call them by name.

2. No matter what you do for them, it is not enough. Indeed, all humane efforts are barely adequate to compensate for the privilege of waiting on them hand and foot.

3. You rarely see a cat walking outside of the house with an adult human being, and it can be safely said that no teenager in his or her right mind wants to be seen in public with their parents.

4. Even if you tell jokes as well as Eddy Izzard, neither your cat nor your teenager will ever crack a smile.

5. Neither cat nor teenager shares your taste in music.

6. Cats and teenagers can lie on the living-room sofa for hours on end without moving, barely breathing.

7. Cats have nine lives. Teenagers carry on as if they did.

8. Cats and teenagers yawn in exactly the same manner, communicating that ultimate human ecstasy – a sense of complete and utter boredom.

9. Cats and teenagers do not improve anyone's furniture.

10. Cats that are free to roam outside sometimes have been known to return in the middle of the night to deposit a dead animal in your bedroom. Teenagers are not above that sort of behaviour.

Thus, if you must raise teenagers, the best sources of advice are not other parents, but vets. It is also a good idea to keep a guidebook on cats at hand at all times. And remember, above all else, put out the food and do not make any sudden moves in their direction. When they make up their minds, they will finally come to you for some affection and comfort, and it will be a triumphant moment for all concerned.